D1478535

9.45'

A LIFE FOR UNITY

Sr. Maria Gabriella

Paul B. Quattrocchi, OCSO

A LIFE FOR UNITY

Sr. Maria Gabriella

New City Press

Published in the United States by New City Press
206 Skillman Avenue, Brooklyn, New York 11211
©1990 New City Press, New York

Translated from the second Italian edition *La Beata Maria
Gabriella dell'Unità* by Sister Mary Jeremiah, O.P.
©1980 Monastero Trappiste, Vitorchiano, Italy

Cover design by Nick Cianfarani

Library of Congress Cataloging-in-Publication Data:

Quattrocchi, Paul B.
    [Beata Maria Gabriella dell'Unità. English]
    A life for unity : Sr. Maria Gabriella / Paul B. Quattrocchi ;
    [translated by Mary Jeremiah].
        p. cm.
    Translation of: La beata Maria Gabriella dell'Unità. 2nd ed.
    ISBN 0-911782-77-X : $9.95
    1. Marie Gabrielle, soeur, 1914-1939. 2. Blessed--Italy--
Sardinia--Biography. 3. Nuns--Italy--Sardinia--Biography.
 4. Church--Unity. 5. Catholic Church--Relations. I. Title.
BX4705.M3866Q8213 1990
271'.97 – dc20
[B]   90-34559

Printed in the United States of America

TABLE OF CONTENTS

INTRODUCTION

Her name was Maria, but they called her Maù.* Nothing special. Not even the prestige of novelty. She arrived after the other four: Mariangela, Mariagiovanna, Salvatore and Pietro. There was no certainty that she would even live very long. Before she was born, two of them, the first and the fourth, had already taken their flight during their first months of life.

She did not even have the privilege of being the last. Into the frail nest three more would arrive: Giovannantonia, called Totona, Bartolomeo and Antonia. This last one was still in her mother's womb when they suddenly lost Papa early in December 1917.

Even her date of birth was veiled in uncertainty for a while: March 17, Tuesday, in the parish register; March 18 in the civic one. It was later explained that Papa, obliged to pull a heavy cart in order to feed so many mouths, waited until after the prescribed limit of five days and to avoid the penalty for being late, he indicated the date of the event as the day after the one read. At the baptismal font on March 21, "Laetare" Sunday, she was given only one name, Maria, without the usual procession of other patron saints.

Maria, that is enough.

Maria Sagheddu, daughter of a forty-one year-old shepherd, Marcantonio, and a thirty-five year-old housewife, Caterina Cucca who was called in the town "Aunt Cucchedda." Maria was baptized on a day in Lent that was filled with Easter joy. It fell between the feasts of St. Joseph and St. Benedict and that of the Annunciation. It was not the pastor who baptized her, but the assistant pastor, Father Francesco Corda. The godfather was Papa's "boss," Dr. Salvatore Cucca, and the godmother was a relative, Francesca Fancello.

---

* *Some have disputed the nickname Maù. But it appears clearly and repeatedly in the official text of the sworn testimony for the Apostolic process, published by the Sacred Congregation for the Causes of Saints (cf. #45 + 93).*

On the same page of the baptismal register two days earlier there is a Salvatore Fancello, and following on March 29, a Pietro Mereu Delussa. All are "household" names at Dorgali.

These facts are necessary to verify what took place in the year of grace, 1914, in Dorgali, a typical little town of the Nuorian region, sheltered by mountains and near the sea on the eastern coast of Sardinia.

Twenty-two years later, we will find this "nobody" no longer living between the rugged mountains and the blue Sardinian sea, but among the gentle verdant slopes of the Albano Hills; a half hour from Rome and a few yards from the famous Squarciarelli, at the moment of a decisive turning point in her life. We can easily say that this was the moment of her second birth. It too, was in silence, hidden, and unseen.

We will also see this "nobody" enclosed between the silent and hidden figure of St. Joseph and the silent unobserved mystery of Mary of Nazareth in the shaded background of St. Benedict.

In fact, on April 13, 1936, in the Trappistine Monastery of Grotta (the usual abbreviation of Grottaferrata, a very long name), dedicated to St. Joseph, Maria Sagheddu abandoned forever the confusing character of Maù. She will be welcomed as a novice into the great family of St. Benedict, and to her baptismal name will be added that of the heavenly messenger of the Annunciation to Mary: she will become Sister Maria Gabriella.

Another twenty-five years will pass and the first miracle attributed to the intercession of the Servant of God, Sister Maria Gabriella Sagheddu, that presumably decides her beatification, will take place again in her history between the dates of March 19-25. We are in 1960, only forty-six years after her birth! She will have as the privileged protagonist, a humble daughter of St. Benedict in an old monastery in Sicily.

But let us proceed in order and return to the beginning. A first and second birth were mentioned. But since every birth presupposes a womb, or formative environment, it will be good to indicate briefly the different environments which, adding to and integrating with one another, functioned as the formative structure of Sister Maria Gabriella's personality; the ethnic womb, friends and family members of Dorgali; and the monastic, and at the same time the ecumenical womb of the Trappistine Monastery of Grottaferrata.

That native stock, that monastic community, the ecumenical reality of the '30s, these are like many colors of a prism. Each of them impressed within her a profound and characteristic mark. But none by themselves is able to explain her, just as she did not identify with just one of these.

Having put these three elements into focus, let us proceed together with the reader in the discovery of her character in the hope of being able to succeed in meeting her face to face.

We do this not so much by speaking of her, but specifically by listening to her, through her own voice and the voices of those persons who were most intimate with her.

The need for dialogue is spoken of everywhere, but in reality, most of the time it is to assure space for oneself so that others listen, with little concern for leaving space for the other and listening to them. Even when both parties succeed in having their say, most of the time instead of a dialogue, it is a "duologue," in which each advances fearlessly along his path listening to himself and following undisturbed his predetermined course, impenetrable to the other's monologue.

We all know what irritation and displeasure a zealous and meddlesome speaker gives during a discourse of great interest. He makes a big fuss in order to tell us with his words and voice what the illustrious orator is seeking in vain to communicate to us. He hinders the pleasure and joy of immediate and direct listening, arrogantly imposing upon us his banal mediation, studded with gross errors. In place of a discreet comment, perceptible to the profound attention of one who would desire it, the underlying meaning is reserved to the protagonist, who, by rolling his eyes and sharpening his hearing, restricts us to intuit and catch a glimpse of the words and stresses and gestures.

It is this imposition that I wanted to avoid here at all cost.

Maù is a simple, modest character, who speaks in a low voice, who never intended to have a following, or history, or chronicle. When she writes she basically has only three recipients: her Mama with relatives and friends in Dorgali; her abbess, Mother Maria Pia; and her first spiritual father, Father Meloni.

She has her own magnificent strength of conviction and of expression, and her very clear manner of communication in addition to a shining style that is surprising in certain points for a young girl who did not have contacts beyond her small island center, and whose family condition did not allow her to apply herself to studies beyond the sixth grade, and who presumably never had the occasion to write letters before.

It would be easy to yield to the temptation, even with the best intentions, to superimpose upon her a stronger voice, the structure of a dialectic manner, systematizing her within pre-established outlines, culminating with a little fantasy of some empty descriptions, interpreting emphatically her bashful attitudes and intentions, or even concealing some unaesthetic manner out of love for the cause. It would end not only by substituting for her, by giving our voice and our face, but also by depriving the reader of the right and the joy of one's own search of her personality in the immediacy of her objective data and also of her contrasts. This would eventually end in re-clothing her and recomposing her along the lines of one's own talent.

We have a rich official chronology of her resulting from the testimonies from the "Process" and we have a correspondence of forty-two letters.

The series of episodes is not that of a "model" little girl who from her infancy furnished an abundance of undeniable signs of future sanctity and who had the charisma of edifying others at any price.

Next to accounts of exquisite sensitivity and unrestrainable generosity, there is revealed a rather "sour" temperament, as her mother defined it. She was obstinate, inclined to be untamed and rebellious, critical and challenging. Her flares of anger, not always edifying, surfaced sometimes even during the novitiate, even though they were unfailingly followed by an immediate and strong will to make reparation: the ritual, her sincere *mea culpa* prescribed by Cistercian custom.

Therefore, we will meet her in person, following in an almost kaleidoscopic manner, different and distinct streams or currents. In the first stream are the testimonies, all eyewitnesses, recounted to us in the "little flowers." Behind the scenes of prudent anonymity with its values and defects, the most characteristic episodes of light and shadow give us a knowledge of her unpolished frankness: first, the irritable Maù, then the strong and gentle Maria Gabriella.

We will do everything to set aside every attempt to evaluate or judge or interpret aside from the testimonies. It is supposed that the reader is intelligent and mature enough to do this alone.

It does not seem just to deprive the reader of his or her conscious participation in the "treasure hunt."

The episodes and anecdotes are reported bare and crude, just as they were narrated under oath in the acts of the canonical processes. The anonymity of the testimonies will serve to depersonalize them, even if in some cases it will be obvious to identify the voice of Mama Caterina, or her sister Giovanna, or Father Meloni, or the abbess.

Anonymity behind the scenes does not take away 1000th of its authenticity. The number in parenthesis which follows each "little flower" indicates the respective paragraph of the official acts of the apostolic process; or, if preceded by the abbreviation "ord." is from the "ordinary" process which took place in the diocesan see. Therefore, one hundred percent authenticity.

Episodes from other sources are omitted. They are neither refused nor denied, but given the scope of this present work, they are simply reduced leaving the subject open. Other biographers may want to stop for a more extended study which really adds nothing more to the essence of the person.

Others also may go to the trouble of submitting the letters to critical analysis whether at the psychological, spiritual, or ascetical level. This can be not only useful but valuable. This has been excluded here.

Here we wish to reserve for Sister Maria Gabriella the role which was least congenial to her. She alone will speak in the first person and tell us about herself. I hope she will forgive me.

Thus, the *Little Flowers of Maù* will accompany us from her infancy to her death in four successive phases: "the flowers of the field," "the flowers of Grotta," "the flowers of the thorn-bush," and "the flowers of the rock."*

We will also follow other themes through her letters, guided by her alone in a true and real, although involuntary, autobiography. We see her no longer at Dorgali, but at a Trappistine monastery and St. John Hospital in Rome; the minute descriptions of life in "my Trappistine monastery"; her fully human and warm relationships with "my people"; and finally, her long journey to God: in the first trials and the first phases of the transformation of her character, in the first sincere and simple

---

* *"The flowers of heaven," narrating the major miracle and other significant graces attributed to Sister Maria Gabriella, was added after her beatification in 1983.*

discoveries of the golden time of the novitiate, until the longed for uttering of vows: "my little offering." Then, the abrupt and unexpected turn of events at the hospital generously passed over in silence for her Mama: "upon the naked cross." Finally, in the joyful consummation of the holocaust: "in profound peace."

In this last phase, the strength of the "little victim" gradually lessens in writing of her intimate drama of oblation and love. We will allow the Mother Abbess to reveal them with her brief writings to her Mama, in order to describe the contours of a picture which fades into the mystery of consummation.

Only one totally empty space remains in her autobiography. A void which it will be necessary and dutiful to supply, and which cannot be done except by prudently returning once again to the voice of her abbess.

A total void, which at first sight could stun and disconcert, but which instead is not really surprising, given her character.

This concerns precisely that element which has made her most "famous" and upon which the Lord has mainly turned the attention of the ecclesiastical world: her offering for unity.

Maria Gabriella does not give the least hint, ever. She presumes it. She generously and joyously bears the burden and the consequences. She does not deny it. She reconfirms it, when asked, in monosyllables. For her it is not a question of a logical, coherent, consequential "ingredient" of the totality of her "little offering." Nothing more than a corollary: the theorem, clear and exciting, is already resolved!

Before such an autobiographic void, the biographer will seek to supply it with the little documentation of incontestable data which come to us directly from her and a member of the Anglican Church. There is the concern not to disturb with the imprudent curiosity of a chronicle, the fragrant veil of modesty with which Gabriella of Unity wished to conceal from people's eyes the most mysterious and strongest moment of her encounter with God. She lived and experienced this moment within the dimensions of an ordinary event, in a simple note, even though high, of a long, generous "solo" of donation and praise.

As we discover the mysteries of her personality unfolding on each page and the admirable evolution wrought in her by grace, may we too eventually integrate our own interior listening with a wonderful resonance.

Paul B. Quattrocchi

A LIFE FOR UNITY

chapter 1

LEAVE YOUR LAND AND GO . . .

Much, very much has been written about Sardinia, good and bad, from the strong and incisive pens of those like Grazia Deledda, to the insipid stories of glossy magazines on the foolish escapades of the international jet-set which has taken over the Emerald Coast, or about the mythical bravery of this or that bandit castled on the Sopramonte.

Here there is no desire, nor does it seem the case, to pen an essay on the rocks and flocks and customs of Sardinia or Barbagia with single brush strokes of color, or pieces of a catalogue. Here, once affirmed that Sardinia is identified neither with the display of nabobs nor with such bandit episodes as feuds and confiscations, we would like to pause briefly upon specifics which are of interest to our narrative, upon the perennial positive values which form the inalienable patrimony of a majority of the Sardinian people and which, precisely because they do not make the news, are usually passed over. Values, which not only were branded into the character of Maria Sagheddu, but values that characterized the entire background in which and from which she was nourished and developed. It was in that geographic point of Sardinia that answers to the name of Dorgali.

Dorgali

The Dorgalians, they say, are a race unto themselves.

The city of Dorgali, situated at a strategic juncture between Barbagia, Baronia, and Ogliastra, assumes a little of the characteristics of all of these places.

It has something of the Dantesque rocks surrounding it, but with a softer bearing like the calm forest of Sopramonte with its wooded vegetation.

It has, in common with Baronia, and in contrast to Barbagia, a greater agricultural openness, without its fertile expanses. It is characterized, however, by its vigorous vineyards from which comes the typical robust and tasty wine of Dorgali, renowned and sought after even beyond the island.

The Dorgalese have absorbed the better qualities: a strong and decisive character (revealed in the physical features of the face and, above all, in the penetrating and willful gaze from very black and piercing eyes); tenacious and laborious industriousness; a marked tribal and strong family sense, in which the austere and rugged father-figure carries out his role as head and provider of the family with full awareness. Because he is continually involved in frequent and prolonged absences, the authority role of the mother is strengthened and has a totally special dimension. She is completely responsible for the on-going formation, economy, and discipline of the domestic community. Dedicated in great part to traditional sheep-raising and agriculture—there is no Dorgalese so poor that he does not possess his little plot of land. The people also have appreciation for craftsmanship and commercial activity, while offering gracious and hospitable welcome to a vast tourist trade. The first historical mention of Dorgali dates back to a census register of 1341, but its history undoubtedly sinks into the haziness of the millennium. The presence of numerous Nuraghi and the characteristic village of Serra Orrios, the ruins of an important Roman road which joined Cagliari to Olbia, the discovery of Roman tombs and ancient consular and imperial coins: all of this confirms that the territory was already densely populated in the Nuragic and Roman epochs.

As far as the introduction of Christianity to this area, it is believable that the relations with Rome and the facility of landing on its nearby beaches permitted that population to know the Gospel very soon. Proof of this Christian presence between the first and third centuries, lies in the discovery of three square stones in the locality of Pranos, above the ravine of Cala Fuìli. On two of these stones, the scholar Taramelli sees "an engraving of the spine of a fish," that could be the "palm" symbol of martyrdom. On the third is sculptured a pointed cross. In the same place a terra cotta fragment with the incision of a cosmic cross was found next to a small tomb, or niche, containing the remains of bones. If, as many are inclined to believe, these archeological finds are valid in documenting a Christian presence, one must conclude that Dorgali and the villages which are found in its territory were among the first centers of the eastern Sardinian coast in which the Gospel was preached.

The ancient parish church was dedicated to Saints Cornelius and Cyprian. This particular dedication, unique in Sardinia, has led some to maintain that the devotion to these martyrs was introduced to Dorgali by some of the African bishops who were deported to Sardinia from Trasamondo in the fifth century. There is very little to give credit to this notion, not only because the above-mentioned church is completely destroyed today, but because it was of Pisan style, and therefore, of the fourteenth century. No traces have been found of a more ancient church.

Nonetheless, the Church undoubtedly, through the work of enlightened pastors, exercised a beneficial influence on the people who, till the present day, show themselves to be profoundly attached to the soundest Christian traditions despite the moral and religious crisis of contemporary society.

It has been learned from an article at the beginning of this century that at least sixteen churches existed within the developed area of Dorgali and ten in the countryside, while another sixteen churches are enumerated of which only ruins remained. The presence of so many churches, many of which were privately built, can be taken as a sign of the profound religious spirit of the Dorgalese, whose piety is generally recognized.

Thanks to its pleasant geographic position, to the fertility of the soil and, above all, to the intelligence and industry of its inhabitants, Dorgali has been one of the most important centers of the diocese of Galtellì throughout the centuries. It was joined to the Archdiocese of Cagliari in 1495. When plans were initiated in the second half of the 1700s to reconstruct the ancient dioceses, it was thought that Dorgali would be the new See, but then Nuoro was chosen because this village is located in the geographic center of the diocese.

A mariner's city since its most remote origins, Dorgali never faced the sea. It is separated from it by the cliffs of Monte Bárdia which rise solemnly from the Gulf of Orosei, while the slopes towards the western side of the same mountain range gently hold the cheerful city in its lap. This position wisely protected the town throughout the centuries from the treacherous raids of sailors.

The beach and port of Dorgali, and its very clear sea water, are therefore beyond Bárdia. They constitute the little tourist center of Cala Gonone (famous for the Grotto de Bue Marino [Grotto of the Sea Ox]), only recently separated from the parish of Dorgali. In order to have access to the sea, the Dorgalese tunneled through the mountain. The tunnel is not easily accessible and is reserved for pedestrians and animals. In the event of pirate raids it was sufficient to block the hole with a few boulders in order to discourage any notion of conquest. It was by this mule-track that Maria Sagheddu also went with her girl friends to enjoy the sea. Only in 1928 was it closed because further downstream there is a new large tunnel that opens unexpectedly upon the blue expanse in a splendid panoramic road and unravels itself in large curves which connect Dorgali with its port, five miles away. Dominated on the southeast by the hill of Carmel on which was hewn a statue of the Redeemer giving his blessing; open to the west towards the expanse of the Sopramonte and Nuoreses, Dorgali gravitates around the main Church of St. Catherine half way up the slope which is accessible by very narrow and steep streets. The only parish in the town, today, for many reasons, it is not the pulsating heart and nerve center it was fifty or sixty years ago.

But even today, in the '80s after twenty painful years of the earthshaking post-conciliar era, there is something in the parish of Dorgali that reveals the mysterious strength of a profoundly lived tradition of faith and grace: the faithful's daily participation at community prayer and the generous vocational response. On ferial days the parish church of St. Catherine is filled twice for the two morning Masses. All the faithful actively participate in the celebration of the Eucharist. They remain a long time in prayer before and after Mass. Many people read the psalms or meditate on the biblical texts of the day's liturgy, while ordinarily no less than two priests are in the confessional. As far as vocations are concerned, the parish community of Dorgali at the present time has provided twenty-one priests, sixty-four religious women, and four seminarians.

The Call

This is the atmosphere in which Maria Sagheddu was born, grew up, and matured. This is the parish in which she was baptized, and the same baptismal font is still there. Here is the confessional where Father Meloni listened to and counseled his spiritual daughter. This is the pulpit from which she heard the message of the word of God. This is the main altar to which she ascended in order to participate at the daily Eucharist, and where she paused for a long time to pray "between two lions." She grew up fifth among eight brothers and sisters, in a modest but not poor family. "Misery uneducates, but poverty educates!" Maù often experienced suffering. It formed her more than the passage of time.

She had to roll up her sleeves very early and commit herself completely to helping, under the wise and firm guidance of her Mama Caterina.

The festive—and laborious—joy of the three cradles which had followed Maria's birth in a steady rhythm (Giovannantonia in 1916, Bartolomeo in 1918 and Antonia in 1920) was overshadowed, in the fullness of her childhood between her third and eighth year, by the still more measured rhythm of the visits of Sister Death, in the notorious Spanish fever. Several were its victims in those years: in 1917 her maternal grandfather; in 1919 her little brother Bartolomeo, followed only fifteen days later by her father who was not yet fifty; in 1920 her grandmother Maria; in 1921 her little sister Antonia who came to light just a few months after the sudden death of her father. But the detachment which wounded her most profoundly, because she was more mature and more exposed to suffering, was the loss of Giovannantonia, born three years after herself. It was she who grew up beside her, to whom she had been sister, mama and nurse. The brief existence of Giovannantonia—short of the threshold of seventeen years—was spent completely under the sign of frailty, illness, and suffering. With a gentle sweetness she ended her meek way of the cross, in an adolescence not yet blossomed, precisely on St. Catherine's day, the feast of the parish and of her Mama, November 25, 1932.

Maria, by now nineteen years old, felt the blow very strongly, but in order not to increase her Mama's burden which was already so laden with sorrow, she enclosed it in silent sorrow.

In what circumstances or for what motives did Maria have her crisis of faith, or how much did she lessen in "religious spirit"? We do not know.

It is certain that at a specific moment—alas if this moment does not arrive!—she experienced the crisis of passing from a faith of relatively familiar customs and a religious practice of ancestral habits, to a strictly personal and responsible response. There was a block. A typical attitude of contradiction.

Like Teresa of Avila and Thérèse of Lisieux, it is far from a yielding to evil; although in later years this adolescent experience she suffered will justify her sense of unworthiness and compunction. Perhaps from this sense of guilt, but perhaps much more from a search for authenticity and personal discovery, she reduced her religious practices to the essentials. She refused to enroll in the parochial Catholic Action. This gave rise to worry on the part of her Mama and surprise among her companions in a community — and an era — in which every good and honest girl, from an innate and religious feeling automatically and obviously was drawn by the centripetal force of the parish, and unfailingly joined, with greater or lesser involvement, an association which at that time was almost exclusively identified with the Young Women of Catholic Action.

It was precisely on the subject of committing herself that Maria waited for clarification, an interior decision, an interior voice, for it was not enough for her that it come from outside. But in what appears to be resistance and refusal before an obstacle, neither she nor the other realizes that her own specific personality is already taking shape. It does not admit of half-measures. Her very personal form of spirituality issues from a profound sense of her own unworthiness, and will accompany her from then on, but without a shadow of complications. It more or less flows unconsciously from her sense of the Absolute and from the relative conflict from her evident need of authenticity, from that instinct of "all for all" which will characterize her rapid ascent, and which reveals — looking at her today — the unmistakable presence of the Spirit's mysterious action which prepared her for her vocation.

She does not refuse God. She perceives beyond the common awareness of the parish. She intuits the all of God and foresees the irrevocable demands of the love of the "hidden God." The Spirit makes her adolescent soul understand that life is a marvelously serious thing, that God is a friend, immensely merciful but terribly demanding, with whom one cannot cheat nor play hide-and-seek. And for a moment, for a long agonizing moment, she is afraid. She is afraid of becoming involved with God, of not having the ability, of not responding to the very depths. It is not God that she fears, but herself in comparison with God; not being able to love him as she should to the very depths. Her fear is not that of Adam, but that of Abraham, of Moses, of Peter, "Lord, depart from me, a sinner."

Maria does not know, and even less do the others, that precisely during this experience of apparent refusal and temptation to flee, there is maturing within her the sacrificial vocation that will be the dominant theme of her entire life. I said, no one knows it, but that is not exact. The Lord had already predisposed the suitable instrument for the opportune moment. Instrument, not artisan. Not a genius, not a "one of a kind," but simply a pious zealous priest, a seeker of God, a faithful witness. It was the young — not too young — assistant pastor of Dorgali, Father Basilio Meloni. It was he who understood Maria's anxiety and hesitation, who foresaw God's designs upon her, and helped Maria to understand God and to say yes to the Absolute.

There were two priests in the parish: the Pastor, Father Giovanni Antonio Mura, cultured, learned; and his assistant, Father Basilio Meloni. The pastor united doctrine with eloquence. He was a good helmsman, but his level of culture and his manner of preaching held him a little aloof from the people, especially the young. It was he who had wanted Catholic Action in the parish, but, as in so many parishes, he had left it to his younger and more enthusiastic assistant to make direct contact with the young people.

There is no doubt that the flawless teaching of the pastor in his homilies and Sunday catechism had its influence on Maria's religious maturing process, for even during the crisis period she never stopped attending Mass in the parish.

But following the hidden work of grace, detecting the reverberations of the Spirit's action in Maria's soul and helping her to decipher them (this alone should be the task of true spiritual direction, especially in the matter of vocation), this task the Lord reserved for the assistant pastor, Father Meloni, who became her confessor and her guide.

The moment of purification and the circumstances which accompanied it are not exactly known. The fact is that at a certain moment we find a Maria Sagheddu who has set aside the uncertainties, displaced the refusals, removed her obstacle, and begun to open herself with docility to the Lord, and to spend herself without mental reservations.

She enrolled in Catholic Action, attended the meetings

regularly, taught catechism in the parish. She returned diligently to the sacraments. She was seen often and for long periods of time in the Church "between the two lions," absorbed in prayer, concentrated in meditation.

And the events matured quickly.

Already in the parish there was a fine vocation movement, especially in the field of women's contemplative life. Some of Maria's girl friends had already chosen the path to the cloister. They were wisely and prudently guided by Father Meloni towards one community or the other, including that of the Trappistines of Grottaferrata.

In this climate Maria's hour also matured. We do not know exactly on which day or on what occasion. At a certain moment, it became natural to say to her confessor: I feel that the Lord is calling me, and I would like to consecrate myself to him. What do you say about it?

Everything unfolds in a very simple and very gradual manner. Father Meloni waited for her and answered her approvingly. Where do you want to go?

Maria: Wherever you want.

Is a Trappistine monastery all right?

She does not exactly know what a Trappistine monastery is. She knows that some of her friends have gone there, and that they have found God there.

She does not even know where it is. Grottaferrata? Who knows!

She has never left the island. Perhaps not even Dorgali except for some barefoot pilgrimages. But what does it matter? A Trappistine monastery? Yes, a Trappistine monastery.

So many times we waste a lot of words, and we end by saying nothing. And the conclusion is even less than that.

Great things are done in silence, or with a minimum of words. The greater they are, the less they need words.

The eternal silence of God! It expresses itself in the one, eternal, infinite Word: the Word, which is God himself. And when God decided to speak outside of himself, with one single word, *fiat*, he gave life to the universe. Meanwhile the long unending chatter of Eve with the serpent rained sin and mourning and death upon the world.

But later only one word will be enough, the *fiat* of Nazareth, for Mary to be able to give the Savior to the world.

20

And again a *fiat* in Gethsemane, and again one on Golgotha, and it will be the salvation of the world.

After Father Meloni's confirmation, the interior yes becomes certainty for Maria Sagheddu.

Then everything unfolds and unravels with the rapidity of the logic of things.

It is Father Meloni who sees about informing and calming Mama Caterina. It is he who makes the arrangements with the Abbess of Grottaferrata, sets the dates and schedules the trip.

Maria keeps a low profile in all this discussion. She has entrusted herself to God's instrument and allows herself to be guided. It is not her task to organize a trip so new to her. By now she has chosen God and that is enough for her. Father Meloni will think of everything else. She has the photograph made for the identification card, and she thinks it better to wear her Dorgalese costume for the occasion. It is her first and next-to-last photograph, and it must be splendid like her twenty-one years. She must set her day of festivity. She goes to say good-bye to friends and relatives, and is concerned about consoling her Mama, asking her to understand, to accept the gift of God.

And then she leaves — serene, simple, without rhetoric and without drama.

She does not want anyone at the bus since Father Meloni wanted it that way, and she, by now, is already immersed in obedience.

The last good-bye's, and then she leaves Dorgali behind her.

At Olbia, she boards a boat with a more experienced friend to whom Father Meloni had wisely confided her, and then leaves Sardinia behind her.

"Leave your land and go."

It began this way, irreversible, without any fanfare or regrets, the journey toward the Promised Land.

chapter 2
THE LITTLE FLOWERS OF MAÙ

I. The Flowers of the Field

1. We were eight children, of whom Salvatore and I are living. We were all educated in the fear of God. Maria always lived with the family. (310)

2. We lost our father and were forced to go to work during the day. My Papa died in the month of November of 1919, when I was not quite twelve years old and my sister was a little more than five. We didn't have an income. My father was a shepherd and cared for other people's animals. (Ord. 291)

3. They were poor laborers who possessed a little plot of land, because everyone at Dorgali had something. (Ord. 214)

4. She had a "sour" temperament. She was often angry, but usually obedient. She sometimes responded without regard even for me. One time she was disrespectful to me and a woman passing by was surprised and scolded her. (83)

5. She was headstrong, whether at school or at home, and imposed her will. When she got it into her head to do something, she didn't stop until she succeeded in doing it or acquiring it. (Ord. 284)

6. As a little girl she had the defects proper to that age. She was unruly and at times irritable and even cursed. Morally, however, she was good. She was physically healthy and of normal height. She was educated by her Mama, the catechist, and the teachers at the elementary school. She was docile, although at times she would obey grumblingly. She attended Sunday Mass, but did not go to the evening services. (311)

7. I remember from her infancy she was afraid of combs and when her Mama combed her hair she would cry. When her Mama sent her to do errands she said she wouldn't go, but nevertheless went immediately. She went to school when she was six years old

and was a very diligent student. She went gladly, but if she missed something she began to cry. I remember that once she wouldn't move until she was given a pen-nib which she needed. To prevent her crying the pen-nib was given to her by a girl nearby. (Ord. 264)

8. Once at the sheepfold, where her Papa was shepherd, her Mama sent her to empty a bucket of garbage with potato peelings. The young girl tenaciously refused. After being spanked because she wouldn't go, she picked up the bucket and took it where her Mama had told her. Arriving at the place, the girl sat down and waited until her Mama left, but after half an hour she reappeared with the peelings in her apron and dropped them on the ground. (97/ Ord. 43)

9. I remember that she had a rather strong character and was accustomed "to talk back" to her Mama, which showed little respect, but not because she was bad, but because she always wanted to have the last word. (Ord. 234)

10. I noticed only the defect of being somewhat harsh in speaking, whether with her Mama or with others. (Ord. 234)

11. She went to school when she was six years old, and she was a gifted student. She liked arithmetic, above all. One day the teacher Moledda called a boy, Cucca, to the blackboard and gave him a problem to solve. The boy gave the answer and then Maria stood up and asked the Professor: "Does this problem seem correct to you?" "If it doesn't seem right to you, come and solve it," replied the teacher annoyed by the girl's rudeness. Maria left her desk, took the chalk and in a moment gave the answer. (82)

12. From the time she was a little girl she would cry when she could not do her homework right. She also cried once when she was older, because her mother wanted her to dress up to go to church. (404)

13. At school she was one of the first [in the class] and her companions often went to her for help. (Ord. 234)

14. She did very well in elementary school. She was always among the best and also studied at Dorgali. She helped her Mama with the chores. She was also respected by the teachers and well liked by her companions. She was not vain. She was not interested in the affairs of others. She played Tombola* and cards with her companions near her house. She was always affectionate with

---

* "Tombola" is a game like Bingo.

her companions and refined in discussions with everyone. (312)

15. Her conversations were always serious. Sometimes she raised her voice and made statements about things she thought she should disapprove of. She had a contentious spirit. (272)

16. She was obedient, but a little hard-headed and quarrelsome. At school she was different, she helped her companions and had the teachers' respect. Once Professor Murgia gave her a prize of fifty cents for obtaining the material to make two shirts. (270)

17. Her companions also went to her home to ask her questions about the homework and lessons. Her strong point was arithmetic, but she also liked geography and history. (270)

18. She was always promoted. She helped with the family work and even went to the country to gather flax and to carry fruit and do the laundry. (270)

19. The teachers considered her a good and intelligent girl. Among her companions there was one who went to her to get help even though her mother was a teacher. (270)

20. Since I didn't attend school regularly, she taught me to read. (Ord. 194)

21. She had a strong character and always wanted to be right. She was of normal height, robust and gracious. (378)

22. To us she seemed a girl like the others and we never thought that one day we would be called to testify about her. I remember that she joked and laughed with a poor half-wit, but without malice. She came to the country to gather fruit. She was very good at school. She was a happy and entertaining child, but simple. (98)

23. Sometimes she lacked self-control and used strong words even with the nieces and nephews, but I think she did it without malice. (70)

24. As a young girl she had the defect of cursing a little, even at my children. But more than real curses they were expressions of anger or impatience with little oppositions. When I corrected her and told her rather to give the little ones a spanking, she replied that such curses escaped her because of habit and she did it without malice. (Ord. 272)

25. She was a nimble and slender girl, and a little nervous and bossy, but good as a whole. The only unbecoming word that she pronounced was: *Accidenti!* [Damn!] (345)

26. She had a small defect, for example, in moments of

impatience to say: "Hell" and "Go to hell." (Ord. 287)

27. As a young girl she was not very interested in going to church, but in reading romances. From the time she was small, she was a little stubborn; later she was more inclined towards religious things and played cards and Tombola. When her mother told her to go to benediction, she responded: "Go yourself." She was very good in her studies. She was impatient and when things didn't go right she stomped her feet forcefully on the ground. (164)

28. She made her first confession and Communion when she was about ten years old. She was not distinguished from the other girls for her piety, nor did she give any particular signs of being religious. She went to the sacraments off and on. She was a little mischievous whether at home or at school, but in general she was good. (311)

29. She didn't go to the sacraments. She played Tombola with me, and when her Mama told her to go to the evening services, she replied that it wasn't obligatory. However, she did go to Mass. (98)

30. Regarding the sacraments, when I began to know her, she was still somewhat "hard," that is, it was not easy to obey. When her mother, upon hearing the bell for services, invited her to go to church, she often responded: "Leave me alone to play" and most of the time she remained intent on the game. (70)

31. In playing she was very passionate and she didn't tolerate cheating, nor sought to cheat others. Her speech was always correct and even her conversations in the family were very serious. After eighteen, she no longer had outbursts of anger, nor played cards or Tombola, because on Sunday she went to teach catechism and she had to work on the other days. (283)

32. She played cards and Tombola and sometimes, when she did not win, she became angry. She was determined to win and knew how to play well. She only played on Sunday and not because it interested her. She didn't have other amusements. She didn't go to church in the evening because she thought that Mass was enough. (Ord. 284)

33. One didn't play cards during Lent because the mothers wouldn't allow it. (283)

34. She liked to read books and her cousin Monni Antonio obtained them for her. He is dead today. He belonged to the Association of Catholic Youth and brought the books from his

Circle's library. She was such an avid reader that once she began reading she didn't want any interruption and continued even at night, so that her Mama had to force her to go to bed by blowing out the candle, since at that time they didn't have electric lights. (Ord. 234)

35. She read a lot; school books and books from the Catholic Action library. Among the books I remember a pamphlet of devotions to St. Brigid that she read for an entire year. She also read at night and her Mama corrected her because it disturbed her, to which she would reply: "I'm almost finished" and almost immediately she quit and put out the candle. I speak only from personal experience. (317)

36. She did not attend amusements and she had few friends. She liked to study. She had a good personality. When we went to the country together, she put the sack on her shoulders and would not permit me to tire myself too much. She carried the larger load of clothes to the river for washing. I don't remember any defects unless one wants to consider as a defect her repugnance to being seen in public. She was very assiduous at work and devoted at home. (Ord. 388)

37. When we went to gather the pears, we took with us a little donkey to carry the bags full of fruit. It sometimes happened during the trip that the donkey rebelled and lay down on the ground. We couldn't make him get up. Maria would laugh and ask: What do we do now? She didn't become angry, or upset, but waited calmly until someone would pass by to help us. She was very reticent and came a few times to my house. (Ord. 387)

38. Often, returning from the river after the washing, she lightened the load by carrying in her hand some laundry that she had taken from my basket. (347)

39. She was a good worker who diligently took care of all the domestic affairs. (70)

40. She was healthy and strong. She had better health than I. She wasn't afraid to wash even in icy water. Once at the river, she broke the ice and washed with great energy, without fear of the cold. Except for Totona, who died as a young girl, everyone in the family was healthy. (354)

41. She was a good and honest girl, respected by everyone for her good qualities. She applied herself to work. She knew how to sew and embroider, and she also worked at the loom with speed and precision. (146)

42. She wasn't the type to be depressed. She patiently overcame her difficulties. She always acted natural. (299)

43. She was happy, reserved, and dignified even on the occasion of the death of her sister Giovannantonia. (333)

44. Many times I urged her to join the Aspirants, but she replied to me: "Catholic Action should be respected and so when one joins one needs to follow the rule, of which I don't feel worthy." Later when she joined on her own initiative, she became so devoted that you had to call her many times because she did not remember to come home. Once she came to visit me at the shore. In the afternoon she was invited to return on a slow ox cart that went to Dorgali, but Maria preferred to go back on the road by foot in order to arrive in time for the religious service at church. (84)

45. I remember that when I couldn't walk any more I asked her: Maù, will you carry me? She took me in her arms and carried me to amuse me. Maria's Mama suffered from rheumatism during those years, so she went to the country to the thermal waters of St. John, where she stayed for fifteen days. She also went to the beach of Cala Gonone for the sun and sand cure. Maria went to visit her and she also carried me with her. We went twice a week and she preferred to take me because it gave her a reason to return immediately to town. When she attended the Association of Young Women, she was eager to return home quickly to attend Mass, even if this meant giving up a ride in an ox cart. (139)

46. One Sunday she agreed to return in the cart of a certain Sini Giovanni. He was a young man about thirty years old. Along the journey he amused himself by addressing teasing words to Maria, which she however couldn't stand and would have preferred not to listen to, even though there wasn't anything bad. When we reached the tunnel that crossed Monte Bárdia, she heard the bell for Mass ring. She jumped down from the cart which did not go more than two miles an hour and invited me to follow her because she did not intend to miss Mass. (140)

47. I did not have the festive dresses of the Sardinian costume. In order to keep me company, she preferred to stay dressed in her usual clothes even on feast days, and we always entered the church by the side door. (52)

48. She was always serious and reserved. Once she took part in a wedding feast with the Sardinian costume of Dorgali, but

she went reluctantly. She was always strict and refined about purity. (271)

49. We wear costumes for feast days, and when her Mama asked her to put it on, she replied that she didn't want to wear it, and if her mother insisted, she cried. (107)

50. She was modest and didn't like luxury. She had the Sardinian costume that I made her when she was a girl, but she wore it only a few times. She led a retired life. She didn't know how to dance, nor do I think she ever took part in one, unless as a tiny girl. She took part in only one wedding celebration. She wasn't attracted to persons of the other sex, nor did she reveal confidences. Two young men proposed to her, but she didn't want to get married. At first she was confused as to whether she should accept or not the proposal of one of them. But having thought a lot about it for several days, she decided to refuse him. (94)

51. She had no difficulty in the practice of chastity. In our towns it is not rare to meet girls who have an instinctive modesty, and even more this love for purity was alive and integral in Maria Gabriella. (493)

52. Returning to the fountain, she had to cross a terrace on which other men and women besides ourselves stopped. She passed by without looking at anyone, her eyes lowered, and speaking only a few words of greeting. The men admired her and said: We don't even know if this girl has eyes! (125)

53. Sometimes during the winter my Mama invited her to come into the house to warm herself, but she replied: If you have something for me to do I'll come, otherwise I'll stay at home. She would do the things in the house for about an hour and when she finished the work, she would say: Now I'll go. There was no arrangement to pay for her services. My mother asked her what she would want and she answered her that she didn't want anything. But she always gave her something. When she left for the monastery my Mama asked her what she could give her. She replied: Nothing. (126)

54. If they offered her a tip, she brought it home to me and left it on the table. She was very strong and self-controlled. (Ord. 364)

55. She entered Religion healthy and strong. I would make a little bed for her at night when she came to my house to help me when my second child was born. She stayed the entire month of

June 1935. She preferred to lie down on a bag stretched out on the floor, saying that the Lord suffered more than we did. (72)

56. On the occasion of the baptism, Gabriella, who had assisted the mother for a month, was given a gift of one dollar by the godparents according to the custom of the village. She wanted to divide it with my Mama since she had offered to help so that each one would have what she needed. My mother, however, would not accept it, even though Maria insisted. (402)

57. I didn't notice anything exceptional during the time I knew her at Dorgali. However, I remember Maria's patience and perseverance in helping a sick woman in the area, who died of cancer and had a disagreeble personality. (Ord. 296)

58. She even cultivated a friendship with a companion whose behavior was questionable, with the intention of saving her. And in fact, this person succeeded in avoiding evil as long as Maria remained at Dorgali. After she left, Maria continued to think of her, asking news of her in her letters. (Ord. 424)

59. She went to visit the sick and regretted that she wasn't able to visit everyone frequently for lack of time. She paid special attention to a sick woman near her home, who lived alone. I think she would visit her more frequently out of pity for her, because when young she had an illegitimate child. (133)

60. I recall she never refused alms to the poor. When she could give no more, she gave at least a crumb of bread. (741)

61. Once Mama asked her to return home, during the break between Catechism class and the devotions in May, in order to continue the weaving of home-made cloth. She complained a little, but she obeyed and agreed with Mama to go to church for the Marian devotion. (315)

62. To judge her by appearances one might say she was an insignificant girl, but when one asked her questions she replied exactly and briefly. (143)

63. She changed decisively when she was about eighteen years old, and was known for her spirit of prayer. At the observation that she should have been so devout before, she replied that "before I didn't see" the need, that is she didn't understand the beauty and importance of prayer and piety. (Ord. 278)

64. I still remember that at my cousin's house when she made bread, Maria Sagheddu went to help her. It is well known that among us this work takes place at night. The people involved get up at 1:00 A.M. or 2:00 A.M. and before beginning the work drink

coffee. Maria, however, never wanted to drink it so as not to break her fast and so be able to go to Communion in the morning. (Ord. 238)

65. For what concerns me, taking into account all the circumstances, I can confirm that there was a continual progress in her, in which she corrected and perfected her character, progressing to maturity in perfection and holiness. (Ord. 220)

66. After she was eighteen years old she went to the sacraments every day unless it was impossible because of an urgent necessity. On the seventeenth day of each month she made an hour of adoration during the day and an hour at night on another day. (279)

67. After she was eighteen years old she began to meditate and she also made a monthly adoration, day and night. (291)

68. She prayed with recollection, kneeling near the sanctuary steps. One saw that she went to church precisely to pray. (132)

69. Her place in church was usually in front of the steps of the main altar, near one or two of the lions of the balustrade. In adversity she used to appeal to the will of God and she also said according to the custom "pro more e Deus siada," or for the love of God. (327)

70. Once she took part in a pilgrimage to Our Lady of the Miracle at Bitti, and another time to the sanctuary of St. Francis in the rural area of Lula. The distances from Dorgali were about thirty and twenty miles, respectively. She traveled the difficult roads, walking barefoot, either to save her shoes or for penance. (278)

71. When she went into the country she often recited the rosary to which I responded. This happened going or returning, but I quit because I used to get tired and didn't answer her more than one rosary. (147)

72. She prayed always and fervently even at home. I remember one night her brother, returning home very late, found her sleeping in the kitchen with her rosary in her hand. Evidently sleep overtook her while she prayed. (92)

73. She was completely disciplined. She didn't give special signs of self-denial. She allowed herself to be guided completely and gently by her spiritual director, that is by me, and was constant in progressing in the virtues. She enjoyed a good reputation, but didn't stand out for extraordinary virtue. (471/472)

74. In her last years of living at Dorgali she went to confession

about every week and received Communion every day. In this regard, I remember precisely having seen her many times kneeling in prayer before the Blessed Sacrament at the steps of the main altar. I was very impressed by her attitude of profound recollection, without any affectation, but rather with a sense of great austerity. I seemed to understand that in those moments she thought of nothing but the Lord. (Ord. 215)

75. I also remember that as a member of the Young Women she took part in the meetings, was a Catechist, and prepared the children for First Communion. She arrived early in order to stay a long time in church, so much so that her Mama, who before had to correct her because she rarely went to church, then had to correct her because it seemed that she stayed too long. (Ord. 236)

76. She was a Catechist and even used the rod. I remember that at that time Father Meloni was the assistant pastor and once he took the rod out of the classroom, leaving in its place a note on which he had written: "Arm yourself with patience and not a stick." She accepted the admonition with humility and proposed to change her method. (273)

77. The day that I left for the monastery I noticed that she watched from behind the door of her house. When the others left she called me, I approached and she said: "Remember me in the house of the Lord," and she gave me a little holy card on which she had written: "Remember me in the gardens of the Lord." (812)

78. I think the seed of a vocation was planted at the Catholic Action meetings in which the Pastor, Father G. A. Mura, gave magnificent and concise lessons of spirituality. (Ord. 352)

79. Since the Pastor was concerned with the Young Women, it was also left to him to care for the vocations. At a certain point I decided to concern myself with it too. It was then that the case of Sister Maria Gabriella presented itself and she spoke to me of the Monastery of Grotta where she had a friend named Marras. She told me that she would also like to go there. I said to her: You want to go to Grottaferrata, then? To which she replied, Send me where you wish. Then I said to her, "Of course, you will go to Grottaferrata." (Ord. 218)

80. She became aware of her religious vocation through Father Meloni. She never talked to me directly and I corrected her for this. It was in the month of June that Father Meloni sent for me

to tell me of my daughter's decision and he invited me to prepare her things. I told him that we were poor and that it was impossible to prepare everything for her in two months. Father Meloni pointed out that if she were getting married I wouldn't have made objections. (85)

81. I also remember that in those circumstances Maria did not have enough money to prepare her clothes. Therefore, since the family did not have ready cash, she suggested her brother buy her share of the land that she expected from her Papa. Since her brother was a shepherd at Orosei and had saved some money, her mother who had the money gave the price of the land to Maria and when her son returned from Orosei she told him: "You know, I gave Maria an amount corresponding to the inheritance she expects and you can take the land. If you don't want it, sell it." And her brother approved of what their Mama had done. (151)

82. But then her brother yielded to her desire and gave her fifty dollars for the journey. (85)

83. Some time before, Magdalene Fancello had left to become a religious. She became Sister Rosa and is now deceased. On that occasion, her Confirmation sponsor told Maria: "If you don't have anything else to do, you can go to the convent too." "It's enough for God to call me," Maria answered her, "and I'll go immediately." "It's not God who calls," the sponsor replied, "but you who put this idea in your head." Later her sponsor repented of these inappropriate words. (85)

84. When she said that she wanted to leave the world and be a religious, I found it hard to believe. Nevertheless the change that had come about in her life was very remarkable. When I asked her if it was true that she would be a religious, she didn't make much of it. She didn't deny the plan to my father and he told her, "A year won't pass before you change your mind." (275)

85. She spoke to me of her intention to be a nun about a year before. And when I asked her the reason for her decision, she replied, "I've been thinking about it for some years and before deciding I wanted to reflect a great deal." I asked her where she intended to go and she responded: "I'll go where my confessor sends me." (128)

86. She was prudent in choosing her state of life and consulted me on the proposal. I don't know if she had talked with others.

Her mother learned of it at the last moment. Before making her choice she prayed to the Lord for a long time. (468)

87. She responded promptly and generously to her vocation and only for supernatural motives, in order to completely and always belong to God. She was indifferent as to which Order. Since I knew the Trappistines I proposed that Order to her and she gladly accepted it. She left her family without tears or regret, with a complete and perfect detachment, encouraging her Mama who greatly grieved over her daughter's departure. (469)

88. When I heard that she wanted to be a Sister, I almost didn't want to believe it, because even though she had improved since joining Catholic Action, she didn't seem to me to be the type called to the convent. (Ord. 287)

89. She decided to be a nun because she felt called. She was ready to go to any institute, without any preference, confiding herself to the choice of her confessor. (275)

90. Outside of the occasions for spiritual direction I had very rare opportunities to meet her, whether because of the great work that absorbed me as a priest, or because in general the pastor was concerned with the women and young girls and because they are by tradition retiring and reserved. (Ord. 213)

91. Once she came to my office to finalize her decision and to take definitive steps for her departure. From what I remember, it was the only time that she spoke explicitly of her decision with me. (Ord. 213)

92. When my father learned that she was leaving for the convent, he said to her: "Go, go, we won't talk again. I bet that a year won't pass before you will have already changed your mind." After two years, Maria, remembering that false prediction, wrote her mother to tell her uncle that two years had passed and she had not changed her mind and that, if it were possible she would have made up for the past years in the world. She advised my mother to offer the Lord a son also to join the Trappists. (Ord. 287/275)

93. When the day of her departure arrived, and she said good-bye to my father, he said, "When will you return, Maù?" She replied: "Uncle Cyprian, we'll meet again in heaven, but never again on this earth." (144)

94. She left with enthusiasm and tranquillity. My brother Salvatore was not happy that she became a nun, because he thought it was a disgrace. All the rest of us were happy. (314)

95. She left dressed in the Dorgalese costume, with a bodice, long skirt and kerchief embroidered and with a fringe. It was my last chance to embrace and kiss her, but I didn't accompany her to the bus because she wouldn't allow it. She left full of joy. (355)

96. A girl-friend of hers said she would go to the boat to say good-bye, but she replied: "I would like it too, but you shouldn't come." When she was asked why, she replied: "Because Father Meloni doesn't want it and we have to obey." (Ord. 226)

97. I remember that the day she left I cried when I said good-bye to her. Maria asked me why I was crying and said: "Why are you crying, aren't you worthy to have a daughter as a Sister?" And then I told her: "Go with God and He will help you." I resigned myself and said: "Rather than return home, God will take her to heaven." Only a cousin accompanied her to the bus in order to carry her suitcase, because Father Meloni did not wish that many people would see her off. (86)

chapter 3
BUT WHAT IS THIS TRAPPISTINE MONASTERY?

The point of departure is always the same: "If you want to be perfect . . . " "whoever wants to come after me . . . " "leave your land. . . ."

The invitation of the Master, beyond the sporadic possibilities, is constantly projected into human history.

In the beginning is the immediate response of those he "wanted," Simon, Andrew, the Twelve, the pious women, the disciples, Stephen, Saul. . . . They make the free choice of those who, in the course of two thousand years, leave everything to cling to Christ. They are docile to the divine call and at the same time attentive to the human signs of the times.

From the first community of the apostolic era to the eremitical and cenobitical experiences of the Near East, from Pacomius and Basil to Benedict of Nursia, from Francis of Assisi to Dominic Guzman, to Teresa of Avila, to Ignatius of Loyola, to Francis de Sales, up to John Bosco and Father Orione, finally to the most recent and varied forms of consecration in the world, it is all a successive and uninterrupted free human choice consenting to the "if you want to" of God.

These human replies which, exactly because they are human, always bear, besides the purity and an unlimited yearning for the hidden face of God, the inevitable elements of frailty, poverty, and human limitation with all their consequences of reversals and revivals in the rediscovered fidelity of forever, as well as in the existential fertility of new situations.

Around the stronger and older stumps there is the blossoming of ever new shoots which, attaching themselves deeply to the original roots, express the unchanging vitality with renewed vigor.

This is the story of the repeated reforms of the great religious

35

institutions. We begin with those which interest us most, the fifteen century-old plant of Benedictine monasticism.

Out of reverential loyalty towards those who first had that charism and transmitted it, these renewals generally take the name not of the reformers — many of whom are famous for holiness — but from the monastery or locality in which the reform was initiated and where it was inserted into the history of its own time: Cluny, Cîteaux, Camaldoli, Vallombrosa, Monteoliveto, La Trappe, Montecasino, Subiaco, and so on. It should also be added that the theme of reform in the monastic world has had as its object, unfailingly although with different emphasis, the three points most vulnerable and exposed to usury and decadence: *poverty*, in crisis by the generosity of donations even more than the industrious labor of the monks; *separation from the world*, ensnared by the difficulty of balancing the right and duty of solitude with the charity of hospitality; *the supremacy of prayer*, undermined by the accumulation of commitments even pastoral ones, or diverted by the easy evasions of a manner of devotionalism, ritualistic and long-winded, quantitative and normative, but poor in presence and devoid of contemplative intimacy.

Already at the time of the apostles it was necessary to have recourse to the institution of deacons — the first "reform" at the community level — precisely in order to withdraw the apostles themselves from excessive pastoral obligation, and to restore to them assiduous prayer and encounter with the Word. Thus even the episode of Ananias and Sapphira indicates the first shift of gospel thought from a personal voluntary poverty to a communitarian one, as well as the censuring attitude of the affluent Corinthians who mortified the less well-to-do at the Eucharistic agape meals.

Cîteaux

One of the most magnificent reforms of monasticism was that of Cluny in the first half of the tenth century. In a little more than two hundred years five of Cluny's abbots were privileged with the charism of sanctity: Odo, Majolus, Odilo, Hugh and Peter the Venerable. It was during the rule of this last one that the need for new radical reforms became apparent. The need increased and, among other things, some monks from the Cluniac

Abbey of Molesme left their monastery in 1098, without serious conflicts. In the wild and marshy forest of Cîteaux, in the neighborhood of Dijon, they sought a secure refuge for a drastic return to the sources. There arose at more or less the same time the Camaldolese (1012) reform of St. Romuald (+1027), that of Vallombrosa (1036) by St. John Gualbert (+1073), and the birth of the Grande Chartreuse (1085) by the work of St. Bruno (+1145). [sic, +1101]

In its early days, Cîteaux also had a series of abbots raised to the altar: Robert, Alberic, and Stephen Harding, without mentioning the raid of Bernard de Fontaines in 1112 with the glorious following of his relatives and friends. St. Bernard was still living when the sons of Cîteaux gave to the Church in 1145 its first and only pontiff. He was Blessed Eugene III (+1153), Bernard Paganelli, the abbot of Tre Fontane alle Acque Salvie, near the gates of Rome. He was a spiritual son, even as pope, of the saintly abbot of Clairvaux. One of the more than 300 Cistercian foundations was on the Island of Sardinia, where also the erection of the famous Marian sanctuary of St. Gonario was attributed to St. Bernard's sphere of activity. At the time of the third abbot of Cîteaux, St. Stephen Harding, the administration of land property, the fruit of those donations which initially they had wanted to renounce, created serious problems of compatibility with the demands of a life of separation from the world and of contemplative prayer, and also the motto: "poor ones with the poor Christ" which was the basis of the "Charter of Charity" of Cîteaux.

After the splendor of more than a century completely pervaded by the highest spirituality which shone with the names of Aelred of Rievaulx (+1166), Guerric of Igny (+1157), Isaac of Stella (+1169), Lutgard of Aywières (+1246), Mechtilde (+1298), and Gertrude of Helfta (+1302), this Cistercian branch of the Benedictine tree gradually lost its status by fluctuating between ways to resolve the exasperating problem of a "stricter" observance or that of a "common" one.

The accumulation of legacies and donations together with the diligent agricultural activity characterizing the *labora* of the monks, transformed the majority of European monasteries, Cistercians and others, into true businesses, rendering them indisputable pioneers of civilization, not only on the levels of art and culture, but also of economy and social progress. It is sufficient to recall in Italy the reclaiming and drainage of the land in the Padana Valley. The tenacity and hard work of the monks transformed it from unhealthy marshes into the most fertile granaries and vineyards in Europe.

But precisely this impressive phenomenon of growth ended by transforming the monasteries into real centers of power, very far in effect from the original visions which sprang from the holy mountains of Subiaco and Cassino, or from the desert forests of Cîteaux.

There was an accumulation around the abbeys of human interests, of greed, of ambitions and of conflicts that, on one side, brought the sad phenomenon of *commende* (benefices), in which the huge land revenues of the monasteries were enjoyed by the few privileged ones of the upper clergy or the upper nobility, called "commanders" (beneficiaries). On the other hand, these same abbeys were unequivocally thrown into the field of the undeniable capitalism of great landowners. This involved them directly in the objectives, at first latent then ever more explicit, of the vindications and social revolutions that were fermenting in the subsoil of Europe, beginning precisely with France.

Among the many cases of this overwhelming degenerative phenomenon is the symptomatic one of a twelve-year-old boy, who in 1638 was already invested with full rights as a commander of three abbeys and two priories. Of these three abbeys, one in Normandy was called La Trappe. The twelve-year-old boy honored by such *commende* was Armand Jean Le Bouthillier de Rancé, the godchild of none other than the great Richelieu.

De Rancé: It was he, who twenty-six years later in 1664, following a tormented conversion which began in 1657, divested himself of all his benefices, and after a year of novitiate in the Cistercian Monastery of the Strict Observance of Perseigne, made his monastic profession on June 6th. Immediately afterwards, on July 13th, he received the abbatial blessing. The following day, July 14, 1664, he officially took possession of the Abbey of La Trappe, no longer vested as a beneficiary abbot, but as a regular abbot. From that day on he took in hand the reins of that same abbey, reshaping the men and the walls whose desolation had been heavily contributed to by five-year periods of beneficiary administration. He had some monks come from Perseigne and achieved the most severe and most rigid among all monastic reforms, returning much more to the school of the desert fathers than that of Montecassino and of Cîteaux. Some shade, more or less unconscious, of a jansenistic mentality cannot be denied either. Nevertheless it is without a doubt that he restored a fervor of monastic fidelity of which every trace had been lost for some time.

But upon all these human vicissitudes, in a certain sense so disconcerting, the hand of God traced the great lines of his inscrutable designs of love.

When the French Revolution exploded in all its sacrilegious vehemence, the National Assembly, carrying out Talleyrand's proposal, made a frontal assault on religious Orders. On November 2, 1789 it decreed the confiscation of all their goods, and on the following February 13th, their suppression, refusing juridical recognition of religious vows. But the Abbey of La Trappe, precisely because of its eccentric austerity which made it famous, and the proven witness of fidelity that its monks offered to the members of the inquiring government commission, acquired, within certain limits, an exceptionally favorable treatment, already brutally refused to monasteries and monks much more qualified, beginning with the monastery of Saint-Germain-des-Près, made famous by the great Mabillon.

In fact, the resolution with which the National Assembly in March 1791 dissociated La Trappe from the type of all other religious cases, authorizing its survival on the condition that the monks besides remaining bound only by simple vows would pledge themselves not to accept new postulants, revealed a mysterious and providential guiding thread of hidden divine plans. It was precisely in expectation of and on account of that provision of partial clemency that the Master of Novices of La Trappe, Dom Augustine de Lestrange, overcame obstacles and also the interfering resistance of less enlightened superiors. With a truly inspired intuition, he succeeded within less than a month of that resolution — 1791 — to transfer and reach safety in Switzerland. In the dilapidated buildings of the ancient and abandoned Cistercian monastery of La Val Sainte in the hospitable canton of Fribourg, twenty-two monks from La Trappe came to be for Cistercian monasticism the equivalent of the biblical "remnant" of Israel.

The incredible vicissitudes of this scanty and original group of the most austere nomad monks, to whom other monks and nuns were added, spread throughout Europe – that overturned Europe – and even into the Russia of the Czars and far off America. The reality of the monasticism of Cîteaux survived, even though altered by the deformations of Abbot de Rancé, and worsened by the still more austere and extravagant innovations of Dom Augustine de Lestrange. It was thus that through the surviving monks of La Trappe and the inexhaustible capacity of energy of the indomitable and unstoppable ex-Master of Novices, that the phenomenon exploded which led them to cross the ocean and to take root permanently in North America.

The mysteries of God!

Feminine monasticism did not remain aloof from the Trappist ferment. Already at the time of Cîteaux there was, a few years later in 1125, the first feminine foundation. It was a distance of three leagues from the Motherhouse near Tart. It was followed by a rapid development surpassing in numbers the same prodigious expansion of the men. Just as the same Abbot de Rancé, during the years of reform, had ended by accepting the confirmed adherence of the feminine communities, beginning in 1692 with that of Clairet in the Diocese of Chartres, so too, the reconstruction work of Dom Augustine ended by uniting these women. When the impetuous waves of the revolution subsided, it was again possible to return to work beyond the agitated and convulsive trials of the Exodus, even if not yet in the joyous stability of the Promised Land foreseen in the Concordat of 1801, but subsequently overturned by successive political upheavals.

Already in 1796 Dom Augustine had founded an original type of women's Trappe in Switzerland, at Sembrancher in Valais. He had the generous idea to gather under one common denominator in severe regularity and austerity, along the same line as La Val Sainte, exiled nuns of any Order thrown out of their respective cloisters by the storm of the revolution. This new monastery, congenially entitled "De la Sainte Voloté de Dieu," was the mother cell of future Trappistine foundations.

But when he returned to La Val Sainte between 1802 and 1803 from his fabulous odyssey with his adventurous and valiant troop of monks and nuns, Dom de Lestrange found that the monastery of Valais had been alienated during his long absence. In the same year of 1802, he began to construct La Grande Riedera (Switzerland), a new monastery in which already by November 1805 he was able to install his most faithful Trappistines.

Then the Napoleonic storm broke loose.

In May 1811 Dom Augustine was arrested by order of Napoleon and all the Trappist monasteries which had arisen in the territory of the Empire were suppressed once again. Dom Augustine, through the intervention of influential friends, obtained a type of provisional liberty which allowed him to emigrate to Switzerland. This was followed by a new warrant for his arrest, now accompanied by an order of execution by firing squad.

The emperor resorted to diplomatic means in order to have him expelled from Switzerland. Arrested and imprisoned at Bordeaux, he once again succeeded in being saved and took refuge in America. But once again the mysterious thread of divine Providence wanted to spare the "remnant" of Israel, this time identified, for unknown reasons, with the Trappistines of Riedera and Rosenthal, temporarily authorized to remain in their monastery. When Napoleon abdicated at Fontainebleau, La Riedera was the only open and efficient Trappistine monastery.

In September 1816 a group of Sisters left La Riedera, and after overcoming various obstacles, reached Vaise, a suburb of Lyon, in 1820. They founded a new monastery under the title of Our Lady of All Consolation.

It was at Vaise, in the summer of 1827, that the old Dom Augustine de Lestrange, stopping amidst one of his exhausting journeys, had to surrender to the inevitability of his fate. In his last sermon, he pointed out the almost prophetic prospect of an immediate ending of the rigid reform of La Val Sainte for a more balanced return to the pure austere original traditions of Cîteaux. He lowered his glorious battle flag on the morning of July 16, 1827, the feast of Cîteaux's founder, St. Stephen Harding.

And here too our itinerary comes to a rapid conclusion.

In 1875, the Abbey of Vaise sent another group of Sisters on a foundation to Piedmont at Saint Vito in Turin, Italy.

In 1898, the community of Saint Vito transferred to Grottaferrata, and solemnly took possession of the new site on September 23rd, after a memorable audience with Pope Leo XIII.

And it is in the Trappistine monastery of Our Lady of St. Joseph in Grottaferrata that on September 30, 1935, will come a young unknown postulant from Sardinia. Her name is Maria Sagheddu. She will become Sister Maria Gabriella.

Grottaferrata

When Sister Maria Gabriella entered the small dark Trappistine monastery of Grottaferrata, she embraced a centuries-old severe and rigid rule, minutely codified in infinite details of usages, ceremonies, and observances that everyone wanted to impregnate with the sacred so that this harmony would overflow into every action.

The very strict enclosure, the rigorous silence, the hard work and the austerity of life were oriented toward the perennial monastic ideal: to make the nun aware of the transforming Presence, capable of listening to the Word and receiving within herself the action of the Spirit by means of interior purifications which render her transparent to everything. Concretely what characterized the community of Grottaferrata was its spirit of penance, the embracing of a continual sacrifice at times heroic, and humble faith, within a situation of material poverty.

It is a question of a community certainly not brilliant with intellectual or cultural gifts or exteriorly notable spiritual breadth . . . but there pervaded a candor of faith and desire for God in the simplicity of persons, life, and environment which rejoiced even in the excessively strict atmosphere. The great event which enlivened the day with its prevailing value and gave meaning to every gesture and every sacrifice was the Divine Office. It was the intensity of the liturgical life "with its ceremonies of the heavenly court" as Mother Pia said.

Sister Maria Gabriella found herself in a novitiate filled with many sisters. Besides the meek and angelic Novice Directress, Mother Tecla Fontana, her formation was taken care of above all by the energetic and very human abbess, Mother Pia. This exceptional personality, very rich and full of contrasts, came from the school of Laval. She brought to the modest Italian community a gust of wind of the traditional, and at the same time prophetic, vigorous monasticism. Having deepened the values of the strongest regularity and adherence to the fundamental observance of the Order, she also opened it to a better organization of work and rhythm of life, to economic improvement, while simultaneously giving a new spiritual thrust to her community. Her concern for the formation of the novices tended to animate a new generation that would generously burn with her same passion for a vocation of radical demands and without compromises. In actuality, her ecclesial intuition will also fructify the community for the following decades. Mother Pia pursued, by means of strongly specified structure, the ideal of a gospel focus expressed in a vibrant life of faith, of sacrifice, of profound and unconditional abandonment to the will of God, of coherent and absolute dedication to the glory of God.

She would introduce, patiently and through the suffering and ardent witness of her great character, the ecumenical ideal into the context of a monastic vocation separated exteriorly from the world and from that more subtle and tenacious attachment to self. An offering of one's life for love of the Church, or for the unity of the various Churches and their members as it was then emphasized, was a way to move the hearts of the young women who had come to the monastery to forget themselves and to risk their entire existence on love, entering into the immense game of the divine with the human. Thus, little Sister Maria Gabriella, with an iron-will, picked up the fire that her abbess had ignited. She did this above all by bending her fiery temper to obedience, to the common monastic everyday life in a constant choice of faith and conversion; and then, with her humble and tenacious receptivity, she made of herself a channel through which Mother Pia's desire to be consumed for the Kingdom could be radiated to all around.

chapter 4
"MY TRAPPISTINE MONASTERY"

"I would like you to know all about our life,
but I will write you a little at a time."
(Letter 5, December 19, 1935)*

The numbers to the left of the beginning of each passage indicate the progressive number in the classification of the letters of Sister Maria Gabriella from which the passage has been taken.

1.   *October 2, 1935*

With great pleasure I write to you, letting you know that I arrived at my destination. I arrived here on Monday at noon; but I am staying outside for a few days, perhaps until the end of the week. In regard to the trip, it went very well in the automobile, as well as on the train and on the steamship.

Mrs. Gavina was so nice. She showed me many churches at Rome and took me to climb the Holy Stairs. I am sending you a holy card of this that I took as a souvenir. She also took me to Saint Mary Major and St. John Lateran, very beautiful churches. But the Church of Saint Praxedes is also beautiful. In that church there is a column to which Jesus was bound for the scourging.

Thanks be to God, I am very well and I want you to know also that they have dressed me like a young lady.

I spoke with Rev. Mother Superior and she told me that Sunday will be the clothing of Sister Rosa, that is to say, Magdalene. Remember to pray for her that day, and for me who needs it.

If you heard the singing of the Sisters in choir, you would say you heard many angels and not people.

---

* *The original book gives two different dates for this letter: 19th and 29th.*

Everything here breathes peace and tranquility and I hope with the Lord's help to be very happy. I will write to you again when I enter the enclosure.

2.   *October 7, 1935*

I want to let you know that Saturday evening I entered the enclosure and yesterday, the day of Our Lady of the Rosary, is the first day that I spent completely in the house of the Lord. Yesterday Sister Rosa received the habit and Sister Michael made profession.

It was so beautiful and moving at the same time to see the two young women kneeling there. They were waiting, one dressed in white and with a crown of roses on her head, for the blessing for herself and for the new habit that she would put on; and the other who before everyone proclaimed to be the faithful bride of Jesus Christ for her entire life.

Pray, my mother, that this day will come for me too. I haven't come here to see the sights, but to remain forever as a faithful bride of Jesus. Do not think that because we are in the cloister everything is true that one always hears about this place. For example, that the food and drink is given to the Sisters by means of a wheel. It's not true, for we all eat very well in the refectory all together.

In regard to the place, it's a real paradise on earth. Yesterday I went for a walk and I saw the vineyard which is a marvel because it still has all its grapes. I also saw the vegetables, that is, cabbage, fennel, and generally everything that can be in a garden. Today I wandered through the garden and saw the few flowers that are there now. But there are also flower-beds for flowers of other seasons. There is also a beautiful statue of St. Joseph with the Child Jesus which stands out among the green ivy.

3.   *October 27, 1935*

I've found here many Sisters who all like me. Just think, we are more than fifty.

The day after I arrived here, I seemed to be in the midst of people who until twenty days ago I had never seen, but now I seem to be among persons with whom I was born, lived, and grew up. It is so beautiful to live in the Lord's house. The hour of prayer is set and so too the hour of work in a way that no one does her own thing, and only in the few minutes for breaks can one read and write and also go to church as one wishes. As far as rising, the Novices and Professed get up at 2:00 A.M.; but I and a few other postulants, since we're still in the first months of arrival, get up at 4:00 A.M. Work can be in the vineyard, the garden, and also in community.

As for silence, I tell you it is a very beautiful thing because in this way there is no murmuring or criticizing as in the countryside, but each one minds her own business and doesn't think about the others. If you could see the Sisters speaking with signs, you would surely laugh and say, Oh! what mutes! Mute, yes, but freely out of love for God.

Sometimes even I laugh when they talk to me because I still don't know all the signs and so I don't understand every time. I hope you will like my new name. It is the beautiful name of the Archangel Gabriel whom the Lord chose to announce the great event to the Blessed Mother. . . .

4.   *December 1935*

As for me, I'm very well in health and in every way. Even though our life is cloistered, we can go outside whenever we wish since we have a lot of property.

We are fifty-four. One does not speak except to Rev. Mother and the Novice Directress, and to the others with signs and a smile of greeting. Nevertheless what is necessary can be expressed and we are satisfied.

Some little difficulties arise, but I think that they come from self-love and the difference between my worldly spirit and the religious one that reigns in the community. I hope with the Lord's help and conforming myself to the monastic customs that the difficulties will quickly disappear. For the rest, in the Lord's house the satisfactions which one experiences surpass not only the small problems, but even the great ones if there should be some.

Rev. Mother put me in the choir to chant the psalms and to sing His praises.

I should be very grateful and thankful for this special grace given to me; but you, Rev. Father, can imagine how confused I am. I have never known anything about music and singing. Nevertheless, I do everything possible to study and I hope that Jesus, if He really wants me, will help me.

5. *December 29, 1935*

The Lord's house is a home of peace and love and I am very happy.

Our mission is to pray for everyone, as much for friends and benefactors, as for enemies. And we do not fail to do this hoping that the Lord will deign to hear our supplications.

Now I want you to know how Holy Christmas went. The day of the vigil we went to bed at 5:00 P.M. I seem to hear you laugh and say: "too early." But we rose at 9:00 P.M. and sang until 11:30 P.M. And don't think that we sang short songs. They were the psalms that we sang. Then at midnight the Mass of the Infant Jesus began. It was also sung and Communion was distributed at it. Just think, to receive the Lord before 1:00 A.M. and ask me if this isn't better than to have a blow-out with a lamb and roast sausages as is the custom at Dorgali. After Mass we still sang and then we went to take a little rest. In the morning we heard five other Masses. Does it seem too much to you?

As for me I want you to know all about our life so you can have an idea; but you know that that is impossible to do all at once. I will write you a little each time and this way you'll be happier.

6. *March 29, 1936*

In regard to myself, today I have the happiness of being able to share some good news.

It is news that fills my heart with joy and that I hope will do the same for you. April 13th, that is Easter Monday, will be the day of my clothing, so much desired and awaited by me.

The day after the Lord's Resurrection I will become His bride.

My heavenly bridegroom has also granted me another grace. Rev. Mother put me among the Choir Sisters to sing His praises day and night. This grace has not been granted me now, but from the first day that I entered the community. Knowing that I am little adapted for singing, I didn't write you anything about it, not knowing how it would go. Now it's not that I've succeeded in singing well, but Rev. Mother says that with the Lord's help I'll learn little by little. If you could see me seated at the harmonium studying the chant, you would surely laugh, and I would too. Sometimes I get tired and end by laughing at my stupidity. But then I think that it is Jesus who commands me to do it and then I make another effort.

7.   *April 15, 1936*

With Jesus I go to find and embrace everyone.

Today has been the great desired and expected day.

Let me tell you about my clothing ceremony. This morning at 8:00 A.M., I left the enclosure and went to the part of the Church that we do not enter. Now, you know our church is like that of St. Magdalene, however a little smaller. Where there is the communion rail at the Magdalene we have the grille. It is of intertwined wood in such a way that the holes are no larger than four or five fingers. At Mass and Benediction it is opened, but when the services finish, it is closed on our side with a black cloth in the frame. In the middle of the grille there is a little door the size of two handspans and this is opened in order to receive Communion. From the floor to the height of three feet, there is also a low wall. We are on the inside and on the other side is the altar where the Fathers come to say Mass. We have two Fathers of our Order, the Chaplain and Assistant-Chaplain, who live in a house that is attached to our monastery, but outside of the enclosure. Both say Mass for us every day.

Now, you know the ceremony of the Lay Sisters takes place on the inside, but, being a Choir Sister, I had to go to the side with the altar. Therefore, at eight o'clock was the Solemn Mass said by Father Abbot, who came for the ceremony, because only he can celebrate this. After Mass he preached a sermon just for me, as is the custom.

After the sermon the blessing of the habits took place. This finished, I knelt before Father Abbot who gave me a lighted candle, symbol of interior light, and the crucifix, symbol of faith. After this the *Veni Creator* was intoned and at the end of the first verse we left in procession. In front were Father Abbot and the two priests; afterwards, myself and a young lady next to me who was my companion and carried the candle. Behind, there were other monks and many women who always come to the ceremony. I was dressed in a white silk gown and I had a veil that went to my feet, like those you might see the young women wear sometimes at Dorgali who are getting married. As I described it we had arrived at the enclosure door where the community was waiting for me.

Rev. Mother was at the door and asked me what I asked for. I had to respond: God's mercy and that of the Order. Then the Father Abbot said a few words commending me to Rev. Mother. After this, following our custom she took me by the hand, and we went in procession into the church.

Rev. Mother took off the silk dress and put one of wool on me, that is the one which I must always wear. This is also white, because the Choir Sisters are clothed this way. Then they put the scapular on me. It is a strip of white wool the size of one-and-one-half handspans and falls down in front and back over the shoulders. It is three fingers shorter than the habit.

Over the habit and scapular a belt of the same white wool and a mantle which goes to my feet, just like that of St Thérèse of the Child Jesus. They cut five locks of hair in the form of a cross from my head. They put a white linen veil on me and a headband and guimpe. Until yesterday, or rather until this morning I was dressed in black, habit and veil, and even a cape that came down to my elbow. From now on, I will wear all white. If they had seen me before at Dorgali, they would have called me a little widow and now they would call me *crofaria*.*

After they clothed me as a Sister, Father recited other prayers and at the end of these the *Te Deum* was sung. During this song I was led by the Novice Directress to embrace all the Professed Choir Sisters. Before this, however, Rev. Mother put a crown of roses on me while *Veni, Sponsa Christi*! was sung. I wore this crown the entire day. The ceremonies ended and the grille closed, everyone left, while I remained for a thanksgiving.

8.   *December 21, 1936*

As for me, my health and everything is going very well. When Sister Raphael and Sister Ursula came they told me that you were displeased because I had not written for a long time. You are right, but please forgive me. I had understood that one had to

---

* *A nickname which at Dorgali is given to the women who wear the habit of the local confraternity.*

wait for permission from Rev. Mother and now they have told me that one must ask. Since I'm a Novice, I would have been given permission to do so. After profession, if there is no need, one does not write more than once or twice a year.

Forgive me then, it wasn't because of an impulsive whim.

I promised you the last time that I would tell you how we spend the day and I am fulfilling that promise. Everyone rises at 2:00 A.M., except if one has not been feeling well or has been doing a lot of work. In this case the superiors can dispense her and she can get up at 3:00 A.M. or 4:00 A.M. Only a few do this, however. The community can never miss the appointed hour stated in the Rule. From 2:10 A.M. until 2:30 A.M. we have the Office of the Blessed Virgin and after this, a half-hour of meditation. Then we have the canonical Office which lasts from 3:00 A.M. to 4:00 A.M. At 4:20 A.M. we hear Mass and go to Communion. After the thanksgiving we recite the Office of Prime and then we go to Chapter.

About 6:00 A.M. we go to the refectory to take the *mixto* and if it's a fast day, the *frustulum*.*

At 6:30 A.M. we have Terce and the second Mass. After a forty-five-minute break, in which we read and the novices also study a little, we recite the Office of Sext that lasts a quarter of an hour.

From 8:15 A.M. until 10:45 A.M. we go to work. After a short break there is None and lunch at 11:30 A.M.; as soon as we are done, we walk for a half-hour if we have worked in the house, and if not, we can read, study, or go to church. On Sunday, Monday, Wednesday, and Friday after the walk we have class, that is an explanation by the Novice Directress on the Rule, the customs or other similar things.

From 1:30 P.M. until 3:45 P.M. we go to work again. At 4:15 P.M. Vespers begins and after fifteen minutes of meditation, we go to supper or collation when it is fasting. After another interval, we have ten minutes of reading in common and this finished, we go to church to recite the Office of Compline, after which we can no longer talk not even with superiors. We go to bed at 7:00 P.M. On Sunday, since part of the Office is sung at night, we rise at 1:30 A.M., and on big feasts we rise at 1:00 A.M. because everything is sung. This schedule is for the Choir Sisters only,

---

* The mixto *(little breakfast)* and frustulum *(collation) are ancient monastic terms for light meals.*

because the Lay Sisters don't take part in all of the Office and so they have more work and less intervals. It would seem that getting up at 2:00 A.M., the day would be very long, but instead it seems like it has just begun and it is already at the end.

I will pray for you during Communion which we will receive at midnight, and also during the Office that will be completely sung. It is my turn to sing the *Gloria in excelsis Deo*. I'll be a little off key, but, patience; the Infant Jesus will accept it just the same.

9.   *March 28, 1937*

I am very happy. I enjoy excellent health. This air seems made just for me. There is nothing more I could ask of my superiors.

11.   *June 9, 1937*

I received the habit on April 13th of last year. The profession, that with God's help I hope to make, cannot be made before the end of one and a half years of novitiate.

12.   *July 31, 1937*

I know that my Sisters who are in the monastery with me are equally happy, and even though we cannot talk, we love one another very much.

14.   *October 10, 1937*

I want to tell you some news that I hope will make you very happy, as it fills me with joy. I have been accepted for profession. It will be on the 31st, the feast of Christ the King.

17.   *October 10, 1937*

The monastery is truly a nest of souls who want to live with Jesus. He has taken me from the world and transplanted me into his garden. These blessed walls protect us not only from the maliciousness of the world, but also from its profane glances.

18.   *November 2, 1937*

The ceremony took place a little after eight o'clock, not in a solemn manner, because it is that way only at the clothing and perpetual profession which will be three years from now. They changed my veil and scapular from white to black. The cincture, instead of wool, is now of leather and goes almost to my feet. The cape was substituted by a cowl which is a type of garment without any form and with large sleeves, large like Saint Maurus wore, as I saw only at Dorgali, but ours is white. We had four Masses, two by Abbots of our Order who are also bishops [*sic*]. After the ceremony there was a solemn Mass with three priests, at which I received holy Communion. Have you ever seen even the richest and noblest couples at Dorgali who would have had such a solemn Mass for their wedding with more than fifty close friends praying for them, and not people who just came to feast and get drunk? And yet, I, the lowest of all, had it. I was asked if I wanted to accept Jesus as my model and bridegroom and I read the formula of profession. I signed it in the middle of Choir and attached it to a cross.

22.   *April 21, 1938*

After profession we are not permitted to write but twice a year; but don't be sad, because in case of necessity whether on your part, as well as mine, the superiors can give permission just the same. There is no rule for you and so you can write whenever you want.

28.   *July 6, 1938*

People of the world say that we are egoistic since we close ourselves in a convent and think only of ourselves. It is a lie. We live a life of continual sacrifice to the point of immolation for the salvation of souls.

30.   *July 21, 1938*

But if it is so beautiful to live in our Monasteries, in this house of the Lord, it is even more beautiful to die here. Just think, my Mother, that for each Religious that dies, whether Choir Sister or Lay Sister, they have to say thirty Masses in succession, without counting the sung Mass and the other funeral prayers.

Each Choir Religious has to recite the Psalter, that is one hundred and fifty Psalms, for the deceased. The Lay Sisters have to say one hundred and fifty Paters or Misereres and in every monastery of the Order each nun and monk has to say three *De Profundis*. In the Monasteries of the Fathers a Mass for all the deceased of the Order is said every day, and so we have the certainty that we will be prayed for perpetually. But not only we enjoy so many privileges, but also our relatives. The entire month of September is consecrated with special prayers for our deceased relatives, friends, and benefactors of the Order.

There is also an Office during this month: Mass and solemn Vespers, and every religious has to say ten Psalters, one thousand five hundred psalms for them. With all that, doesn't it seem beautiful and sublime to die in our Order?

32.   *September 22, 1938*

It is truly a great fortune to live in the monastery, where all the actions, even the most lowly, or even when we are recreating, when it is commanded by obedience, cause great merit.

chapter 5

THE LITTLE FLOWERS OF MAÙ

II. The Flowers of Grotta

98. Upon her arrival at Grotta she was received by the superior Mother Pia. I saw her because Mother Pia took me to the parlor to greet her. I had been gathering walnuts, and so I had black hands. Mother Pia said, "Look, what hands!" She replied, "Oh! what joy, Rev. Mother. I like this, because outside they say that nuns don't do anything. Instead they work, and I'm happy." (821)

99. At the beginning of her religious life this impatience, which was her predominant fault, had not yet completely gone away. (861)

100. At the beginning she showed a little annoyance if the Novice Directress or Rev. Mother did not receive her immediately in order to avoid losing time. Later she corrected it completely. (504)

101. I remember that waiting at the door of Mother Abbess, she knocked on the door and, not receiving an answer, she knocked at least six times, then gave the door a strong punch and left angry. (Ord. 45)

102. We were together the Professed and the Novices, when I saw her impatient with the Novice Directress because she had received a knife that was too small to peel with. She became all red and fumed with rage. (Ord. 45)

103. She had a tenacious, strong will. She was a little irascible by temperament, which however she powerfully dominated. (537)

104. The Novice Directress, speaking with the superior as she later recounted to me herself, said that Sister Gabriella had a very strong spirit of criticism, but that "now it was very much corrected." (155)

105. Another time, the Assistant Directress made an observation to Sister Gabriella in the refectory because she didn't eat

bread. At this Sister Gabriella annoyed replied to her, "It's not up to you to make this observation to me. I eat what I want." They both separated upset. (154)

106. She had a personality easily given to anger and dominating others. It was later improved. I can personally verify this. (356)

107. Initially she was a little vivacious, but then she became very humble and patient. She corrected herself immediately in the beginning. (508)

108. She practiced innumerable acts of patience during her illness. I saw her acts of impatience two or three times. She did not offend the Sisters. She became bright red, contained herself and fled. Or sometimes she would fall down on her knees and ask pardon. An embrace followed and it was all finished. (538)

109. I taught her to work in the book-bindery. When she was corrected, she never made an excuse. Despite the fact that I was very demanding, there was never anything to object to with Sister Gabriella and I never found her harsh. She wasn't a "cream-puff." She had a strong character that she fought and conquered. (Ord. 93)

110. Once in the bindery I noticed a sign of impatience. There was an old Mother who had put the book badly in the screw-vice, and she made a gesture as if to say: "It's not right." She immediately realized she had not done well, she knelt down and beat her breast. (824)

111. We also went to the bindery together. When the bell rang at the end of work, Mother Cellarer had told us not to leave the room in disorder, to return everything to its place, which took time. The Novice Directress, on the other hand, corrected us because we were always late to the Novitiate and we had to study the Rule, the Customs, etc. They were two things that couldn't be reconciled, although she tried to do her utmost to put everything in order. I, contrary to the Rule, crossed through the cloister garden and ran through the cloister in order to avoid the scolding. She instead arrived slowly and solemnly, contrite and reserved. She was ready to receive her correction in a spirit of humility without transgressing the Rule in the least. (237)

112. Both Mother Armanda and Sister Gabriella wanted a Sister to be assigned to help them: Mother Armanda for the work in the vineyard, and Sister Gabriella for the bindery. Mother Armanda insisted so Sister Gabriella yielded and went to the

book-bindery alone. In the discussion Sister Gabriella was a little heated, but she submitted when the Novice Directress touched her hand to warn her to give in. (776)

113. I remember she smiled and gladly did any kind of work, without showing that she had a preference for work in the vineyard, orchard, or bindery. (Ord. 505)

114. She was with me at the wearisome work in the vineyard. She offered to do the hardest work and was very generous. If she knew of a job that was not finished or forgotten, without saying anything, she would try to finish it in a spirit of charity. (Ord. 26)

115. She was obedient and always submissive to her superiors. When we worked together she was one who never left tools or garments at her place. She put everything away. (844)

116. She spoke little. She was not very effusive, but very efficient. (Ord. 92)

117. Once during the postulancy, I saw that she was limping and I said to her: "What's wrong that you walk like that?" "Perhaps it's the shoe. It's nothing," she replied. On the contrary, she had blisters that hurt her very much. (725)

118. I remember that when she went to the vineyard or garden, she returned carrying the heavy loads on her head and without ever stopping to rest. (146)

119. Mother Pia wanted her to learn to play the harmonium since she was tone-deaf. She learned well. After her turn for the Invitatory in Choir, Mother told her she did well. She replied, "No, I did badly." After Mother repeated her statement and received the same response, the Mother Abbess said: "Yes, yes, you think what you want," and the Servant of God immediately made the *mea culpa*.* (605)

120. One day everyone went to work in common to pull weeds. I was near Sister Gabriella. We put some rags on our hands so as not to get stuck by the nettle, while she pulled them with bare hands. I said to her: "Why don't you cover your hands?" and she said, "Oh no, one needs to give some little flower to the Lord" and she continued with a sweet smile. (836/Ord. 525)

121. When she wrote, her Mama passed on her letters to me and we were surprised that she said so much, because she seemed to be a different person. My brother-in-law observed that the

---

* *A gesture of striking one's breast as a sign of repentance and asking forgiveness.*

sense of these letters was of a level superior to Sister Maria Gabriella's ability, for she only had elementary studies. (Ord. 390)

122. Once when I wrote her asking for prayers, she replied exhorting me to have faith. I remember that she was corrected by her superior for this, because she had presumed to give counsel to a priest. So she wrote me again asking pardon. (Ord. 222)

123. One day Rev. Mother Abbess to my "if" and "but" said to me: "The Community thinks you are the most happy and content and it is not always so in reality. On the other hand, Sister Gabriella is considered the most sad and humiliated, but on the contrary she has a soul full of joy, peace and gratitude towards God and the Community." Shortly afterwards I noticed a change in her: all at once she acquired a sweet, gentle, and serene behavior. Mystery! I learned after that it was imposed by obedience. (245)

124. Before her illness, I was struck by the pallor of her dark face, a little olive-colored. She was of medium height, slender but not skinny, right for her age. She had a voice that was strong, clear, and good range that certainly did not give any hints of a pulmonary disease. I never thought that she might be ill.

She was always prompt to rise at 2:00 A.M., and regularly fulfilled her duties throughout the entire day and the work which called for great physical strength. I would say her coloring was a little tan. It was the Sardinian color, but everything else was fine, and especially her voice was not that of a candidate for consumption. She continued to do her reading in the refectory for a half hour at dinner and a half hour at supper, with a strong voice, for the entire week of her turn. (553-555)

125. She had a little instinctive pride from the time she was a child, but it was later corrected. She said she was and considered herself to be a poor sinner. (370)

126. She regarded herself inferior to the others and a sinner, as I was able to observe. She did not excuse herself if she committed even a slight failing. She did not refuse the most humble tasks. (407)

127. She was always ready to humble herself. She always knelt and said: "My fault" before any observation. (160)

128. She acknowledged herself guilty even when it concerned a general observation. (52)

129. She also knew how to deny herself and understood when others were right. (370)

130. Regarding humility, her characteristic was always the desire to hide herself and not appear before people. (494)

131. She did not desire to stand out, nor was she ambitious in any other way. She worked and did her duty. (302)

132. She stayed at her place. She accepted any task without preference. She was not envious. She was humble and submissive. (337)

133. She was not too vain to appear humble. (337)

134. She went where she could be useful. She would say that her motto was to become a saint without attracting attention and to observe the Rule with the maximum precision. (234)

135. As for the duties, lowly or not, she accepted what was assigned to her. (580)

136. She had a little difficulty convincing herself when they wanted to give her the direction of the bindery, because she was afraid to command others. (580)

137. After profession she continued her simple life as before. I saw her personality gradually become more and more patient. (535)

138. Progress in general was noted and then an uncommon interior recollection, giving the impression of her continual smile, full of peace. (687)

139. I knew, talking with the superiors, of her state of constant aridity and this made it more difficult to practice virtue and our life of long choral prayers. (688)

140. Her simplicity in the common life was manifest. She never asked for anything and she never refused anything. (884)

141. She channeled her natural strength of character towards mortification of her temperament and the acquisition of virtue for her sanctification. (491)

142. She faced difficult things with simplicity. She tried. (574)

143. She always had her rosary at hand. (161)

144. Very tactful, careful not to displease anyone. (668)

145. She was simplicity personified. (669)

146. Very sensitive, perhaps a little excessive, but not at the confessional.

Scrupulous in the preparation of the Office. She ascribed to the Trinitarian Work of Aiaccio and to the Work of the Far East for the conversion of Japan and China, like the entire Community. (559)

147. She was faithful to Communion on the 15th of each month for China and Japan. (564)

148. She spent all her free time before the tabernacle. (839)

149. She manifested a true devotion towards her superiors. She never sought help, advice, suggestions outside the monastery. (883)

150. She accepted in a completely natural way the difficulties and privations of life. She lived a peaceful life, but without special prominence. (299)

151. She never complained about her poverty nor desired to be better. She was born poor and considered herself rich in the midst of privations. She was always moderate and not wasteful. (334)

152. She observed great religious poverty. She was never ashamed that she came from a poor family. I was Clothing Room Sister, and I can say that she wore clothes mended to the maximum, belonging to another Sister who had died years before. She never used the clothes from her Clothing and Profession except on those days. She went to the hospital in a patched, but clean, habit. (575)

chapter 6
"MY LITTLE OFFERING"

3.   *October 17, 1935*

Pray to the Lord that He would help me not only to
understand what they tell me, but also to put the teachings into
practice, that is to obey the superiors and to observe exactly the
rule of my institute and thus become a saint before God.

4.   *December 1935*

The silence that is practiced here is good for me and I find it
much better than worldly chatter.

The Lord shows Himself ever more merciful with me, even
though I am most unworthy and not good in corresponding to
such goodness.

5.   *December 29, 1935*

Thank Him also, my Mother, since I'm not able to do it
enough. And pray always so that He might help me soon to
become a bride worthy of Him. And tell Him to make me suffer
death a hundred times rather than leave these holy walls, where
I have been welcomed with so much love.

6.   *March 29, 1936*

It seems somewhat incredible, yet it is true. Have you thought,
O my dear ones, of this unsurpassable gift? He, my Jesus, could
have chosen many other souls who were much more loving, more
pure, innocent, more worthy. But no, He wanted to choose me,
even though I am unworthy.

After so many graces, so much love and so many favors, how
could I not melt in love for my Bridegroom?

7. *April 13, 1936*

I made the wedding covenant of eternal love with Jesus. He will be all mine and I will be all His. He, my Creator, has not disdained to call me His bride. Although I am His miserable and unworthy creature who has done nothing but offend Him, He has not rejected me, but gathered me to His bosom. The love of Jesus is truly great and no creature no matter how perfect will ever equal this love. The love of Jesus purifies, burns, inflames hearts.

I feel that He has always loved me and that He loves me even more now. I realize that He has favored me in a special way by giving this great grace to me, while He could have chosen many others worthier than I and who would have responded more generously to His love. But it wasn't to be that way. He wanted to make me the object of His mercies.

When I think about this, I am confused at seeing the great love Jesus has for me, and my ingratitude and failure to respond to His favors.

Now I understand well the saying that God does not wish the death of the sinner, but that one be converted and live, because I have experienced it in myself. He has acted toward me as toward the prodigal son.

8. *December 21, 1936*

I do not ask the Lord to free me from suffering, but that He give me the strength to suffer for love of Him everything that it pleases Him to send me.

9. *March 28, 1937*

I live, eat, sleep under the same roof with Jesus and what more could I want in this miserable mortal life? My only desire is to love my God and my Bridegroom more and more, to make myself ever more worthy of Him and to become a saint. Don't think that I mean a saint to be put on the altars for that would be presumptuous on my part, but I desire only the sanctity of the perfect fulfillment of my duties.

11.   *June 9, 1937*

I enjoy good health and am very happy to find myself in the Lord's house.

If sometimes the thought comes to mind that I could be sent away, it gives me such horror that I flee it as I would run away from a poisonous snake. My heart feels faint at this thought and I would be happier if I were cut up in pieces than to leave the monastery. My only regret is not to know how to love the Lord as I desire and as I should. I feel that I am very weak and indifferent. Nevertheless the Lord not only sustains me, but still fills me with blessing.

I am in Choir because Rev. Mother wanted it that way. I know little about singing, but a lot about being "off-key." Because of this I wanted to quit before my clothing, but Rev. Mother didn't want it, saying that I will learn little by little.

I must thank the Lord for all His blessings, but in a special way for having given me a religious vocation and for having brought me here far from the world and its snares. It is truly fortunate to be a religious because it is not only to be safe from many occasions of sin, but even more, if through misfortune we fall a hundred arms are quick to lift us up.

I confess, however, to have had an illusion. For me, to enter the convent and to become perfect was the same thing and instead I've had to convince myself by experience that it is not so. In order to arrive at perfection I've seen that it is necessary to work a great deal, and that entering the monastery I brought with me my ego and my defects which I have to fight continually. But what does this matter? If perfection didn't cost, it wouldn't be worth anything. The Lord who has put me on this path will remember to help me in the fight to gain victory.

12.   *July 31, 1937*

At certain times it seems that the Lord abandons us and forgets us, but instead it's simply a proof of His immense love in order to see if we remain faithful so as to reward us even more lavishly afterwards.

Regarding myself, I can assure you that I am very well and the more I advance, the happier I am to find myself here. The Lord has truly been very good to me and I could not hope for anything better.

14. *October 10, 1937*

The King of heaven and earth, the God of the universe, wants to take for His bride a miserable and unworthy creature like me.

Yes, I, a poor creature, will become a queen because He desires it. I could never have desired a more beautiful feast for my consecration to the Lord.

Feast of Christ the King   *October 31, 1937*

In the simplicity of my heart I joyfully offer You everything, O Lord. You have been pleased to call me to Yourself and I come rushing to Your feet. On Your royal feast day You wish to make this miserable creature a queen. I thank You with a completely overflowing soul and in pronouncing my vows abandon myself entirely to You.

Grant, O Jesus, that I may always remain faithful to my promises and that I may never take back what I give You this day. Come and reign in my soul as the King of love.

I beg You to bless our monastery and make it the garden of repose for Your Heart. Bless in a special way the superior who has the greatest responsibility before You.

Bless all of my family, and in particular I commend to You my brother and my brother-in-law, make an impression on their hearts and enter them to take possession there as King. Turn Your kind gaze upon our entire Order, and make it a seed-bed of saints.

I pray to You for Your Church, the supreme pontiff, and our bishop. I commend to your divine Heart all of my relatives, friends, and benefactors, my parish and the Association that I belonged to, deign to give everyone peace, joy, and blessing.

I commend to You the benefactors of our monastery and the Sister who had to leave us, so that you may accomplish the expected miracle.

I pray for the Sisters from my countryside: that they can all persevere in love.

Above all I recommend to You Rev. Mother, the Novice Directress and my confessor, that You would reward them for all they do for me and give them the light with which they can guide me in the way You have marked out for me, and give me a great docility in obeying.

O Jesus, I offer myself in union with You in Your Sacrifice, and although I am unworthy and nothing, I firmly hope that the divine Father will look upon my little offering with the eyes of kindness, since I am united to You. I have given You everything that was in my power to give.

O Jesus, consume me as a little victim of love for Your glory and for the salvation of souls.

Eternal Father, show that Your Son goes to the wedding feast today, and establish Your kingdom in all hearts, so that everyone loving and serving Him will be conformed to Your divine will. Give me whatever is necessary to be a true bride of Jesus. Amen.

18.   *November 2, 1937*

As had been decided, the day before yesterday I made my profession and consecrated myself entirely to Jesus by religious vows. The joy that I experienced and still feel is indescribable. The world cannot give this joy and therefore does not understand it either. Only Jesus can make souls feel these intimate joys, which make them forget the pains of this earthly exile and always inflame the soul to a greater desire for Paradise. They cannot explain it in words, but only one who has experienced it knows. Before, I was always afraid that they would send me away and that my desire to belong completely to Jesus would fail; but now I feel certain that I will remain forever in the Lord's house and therefore my joy is immense. What joy, what happiness to be admitted by Jesus to the mystical espousal!

19.   *December 17, 1937*

October 31st I made my religious profession.

I could never have experienced a more beautiful day than the feast of Christ the King for my complete consecration to Him who must be the King of my heart and my soul. My happiness is at its height because now it is no longer a dream, but really true that I have become the bride of Jesus and I am sure to stay forever in His house. The vows are really for three years, but I don't think about this, because they can no longer send me away except for a lack of religious spirit or an illness maliciously hidden.

I thank the Lord that I'm not sick and regarding a lack of the spirit of my vocation, I pray that I may die not once but a thousand times if this happened.

I'm very well in all respects. The interior trials are not missing, on the contrary it would be a joke to think one could be exempt.

I don't have much ability for the Choral Office. In the beginning whenever it was my turn I cried because I couldn't succeed in doing it, but now it is no longer the case. I use all the effort that's possible, and then if the Lord wants me to be humiliated, may His will be done. I desire only to be sanctified in love, in the observance of my duties and in perfect abandonment to God's will. He who has brought me this far will sustain me in the future.

20.   *December 20, 1937*

Even if when I left I might have been in a state of indecision, which really wasn't so, now Jesus has confirmed me more than ever in my vocation.

chapter 7
"TO MY PEOPLE"

1. *October 2, 1935*

How are you? Has the unhappiness passed? I hope so, because you will have to resign yourself and even be content to think that it is a great grace the Lord has granted me and of which I was unworthy.

I greet everyone of you, brother, sister and brother-in-law. Say hello to all the relatives and neighbors, grandmother Francesca and grandmother Michela and also let me know if she is well and if she had the operation.

Greet Maria Fancello, Anna Pateri and Michelangela and Mallena Lai and tell Maria to greet the circle president and sisters and Giuseppedda. In conclusion greet everyone, because if I wrote all their names, I wouldn't even have enough paper. I kiss your hands and ask you to bless me.

2. *October 7, 1935*

Since the day of his departure by automobile, let me know if Salvatore has returned and how he is.

3. *October 17, 1935*

Don't think I have forgotten you, but rather I pray even more to the Lord that He will grant you the graces that you need for temporal and eternal life.

4. *December 1935*

Rev. Mother told me that you have been transferred to Ollolai and so I think my village will have to resign itself to losing you. Even in this we have to see God's will. I congratulate you on this new parish assignment, you can work according to your own desires and with this people you will harvest the copious fruits of your labors. The people themselves won't be ungrateful and I hope that they will respond generously to your loving care.

I must be grateful to you for my happiness. You worked so hard for me and I thank you from my heart, but finding myself so much in debt to you, I don't know exactly how to express my gratitude to you.

5.   *December 29, 1935*

For my part I never fail to pray every day for you and all the family, for our relatives and benefactors, and finally for our country and for the entire world.

Let me know if the mission came that you were waiting for and if godfather Billia and Salvatore have gone to confession. I would also like to know if the circle-groups and religion classes are continuing, or if the village is very resentful about Father Meloni's departure.

6.   *March 29, 1936*

I was unhappy to hear that the village has let the religion classes go down because of Father Meloni's departure. Let's pray to the Lord and He will provide for everyone.

I also desire that you spend this day in festivity and holy joy in order to thank the Lord for all the graces He's given me.

When you go to receive Holy Communion, the little ones too, pray to God for me. Ask Him for the grace of perseverance, so that growing every day in His love I might fulfill all my duties in order to live in perfect submission to my Lord's will. Say a special prayer that I can learn to sing well and respond to this grace. I suggest that on that day you sing the Magnificat with me.

7.   *April 13, 1936*

You can imagine my joy and I'm sure that you also share it. Even more I'm certain that you have prayed for me, as I have prayed for you. Continue to pray that I may always be faithful to my obligations and to my rules, always doing the Lord's will without ever offending Him, and so live happily all my life in His house.

This evening I received your telegram and I thank you very much. I hope that you had a happy Easter and that everyone is well. When you answer me, let me know how Salvatore and my brother-in-law are. I greet and embrace everyone in Jesus when I go to Communion. Say hello to the girlfriends and companions, parents and neighbors.

8.   *December 21, 1936*

Today I was given permission to write to you and I do so with great pleasure. I have received your letters and I am happy to hear of your news and also that Marco Antonio made his First Communion.

And don't think that I've become insensitive to your love. On the contrary my heart has suffered to think that I hurt you, but I offer it to Jesus who suffered so much for us and I hope that you have done the same. If the Lord offers us something to suffer for love of Him, we should be very happy and accept it gratefully.

Tell my cousin Nanneddu Monni and his father that the trial year that they gave me is over, and that I have not changed my mind. I am very happy and would not exchange my place in the monastery, where I dig, hoe, and do everything that comes along, with what I would have had if I'd remained in the world. I would prefer to suffer some martyrdom rather than cross the threshold of my monastery.

Even though I can't talk with you and write to you frequently, I speak of you every day to Jesus at Holy Communion and tell Him to go and console you for me.

Pray for me, that I might soon become a holy religious, His bride in fact and not in name only.

I heard that Giovanna has a new baby boy. I'm glad and send her best wishes that he will be her consolation and a good servant of God.

9.   *March 28, 1937*

For my part I never fail to pray for you. This is one of my greatest duties, and even though I can't write you often, I commend you to Jesus in Communion, which thanks to Him I have never missed, with the exception of two Good Fridays. I'm sure that He will speak to you much better than I could writing these poor lines.

I was glad to hear also that godmother Michela has recovered her sight a little.

When you write me, give me news of your spiritual progress. As for you, I am sure you will continue to go to Communion and attend Mass every day; but of Giovanna, the children and our men you write me nothing and therefore I don't know. Tell me if Father Meloni is still at Ollolai. Tell me if Michelangelo has returned to Dorgali, if he goes to Communion every day and what he thinks.

10.   *March 28, 1937*

Dearest brother,

I want to know if you and Giomaria made your Easter duty. Did you? I hope so.

I remember that when you wrote me last year, you said that you weren't able to go because you were in the country, but that you thought of God where you were. You do well to think of God wherever you find yourself, but it's not enough. Tell me, O brother, if you were engaged and told your fiancé: "I love you, but I can't come to you because I must always stay with the sheep, but I do think of you where I am." What would she reply to you? She'd send you away and she would surely say: "If you are always with the sheep and never come to see me, it's a sign that you love them more than me and you're not worthy of me." Well, God does the same with us. If we turn our backs, He also turns from us; but if we love Him and go to Him with all our heart, He certainly will not be outdone in generosity, but will reward us greatly and beyond measure. My brother, if you haven't yet made your duty, don't put it off any longer, but run and together with Giomaria go to Jesus and He will enrich you with His gifts and blessings.

11.   *June 9, 1937*

I pray for you, whom I owe gratitude, since you have been so interested in me; but on that day I will pray even more and I'll offer my Communion for your intentions.

I was very happy with the news you gave me and especially with your spiritual progress. I hear that you continue daily Communion and that you go to Benediction every day, and so I encourage you, as much as you can, not to abandon these practices. Even if at the time of prayer the Lord seems to sleep, the day will certainly not fail when it will bear fruit.

You told me that Giovanna wants to go to church, but that she can't go because of the children. I understand very well how with five little lively youngsters one can't do what one wants, but the Lord is so good, He's happy even with only good will when we can't put it into practice because of legitimate reasons. When she can, she should go and not omit it out of negligence, then the Lord will not leave her efforts without rewarding them. When she cannot go, she should offer her desire to God and He, in His great goodness, will accept it as if she had really gone. To make up for this deficiency send the older children, in order to show them the right path and to take them away from bad companions. Especially send Marcantonio often, so that acquiring the habit, when he's older he won't quit.

And my little Caterina, who was embarrassed to make the sign of the cross, you tell me that she studied the catechism until she knew it by heart. I'm glad; but why isn't she being prepared for First Communion? At five-and-a-half years old, she could make it very well. I beg you to prepare her at least for my profession that will be after the two years of the novitiate are over. Tell her to make the effort to study in order to please her godmother.

You wrote me that Salvatore is not in the fields. I waited for his reply in vain and that made me unhappy, because I think I can guess the reason for his silence. He didn't do what I told him and so he didn't answer me.

The Lord must have wanted me to be mistaken in this thought, but it makes me unhappy when I think that I am at a Trappistine monastery and my brothers are farther away from God. It seems that they want to be far from Him and I believe that the Lord is not very happy about this. I hope that now he will return home and will write for my profession.

13.   *July 31, 1937*

Dearest niece,

In Mama's letter I found a few lines written to me from you and I'm happy about the news you gave me. You told me that you studied for the catechism contest.

Study always and you will be a true "Good Friend" of the Heart of Jesus. He prefers the little ones. Go to receive Him often in Communion. Don't be satisfied with going to Mass and Communion only on Sunday, but also go the other days since you are still small and can't help your Mama with the work. When you go to church, take my little Caterina so that soon she also will learn to love Jesus. Always obey Mama and Papa and grandmother, for the virtue of obedience is the one that pleases Jesus the most.

14.   *October 10, 1937*

I'm happy that you went to the thermal baths, because this way you'll stay in good health and will always be able to go to church. You told me that Caterina has already made her First Communion and of this I'm also most pleased.

You, my mother, should consider yourself very fortunate that the Lord has seen fit to choose a bride from your family. Thank Him greatly for this favor to you and for this gift He has given to me. On this happy day I beg you to double your prayers and to celebrate as we do in the monastery, because this is truly the day of my espousal with Jesus.

Above all, I encourage you not to be saddened that the profession signals our separation forever. If we had been nearby, you would have been able to come to the ceremony or else visit with me, since visits from relatives are allowed twice a year. But since we are too far away, you must resign yourself and think that this is God's will.

Could the woman who writes [for you], please reread the letter before mailing it? Because sometimes I find unintelligible things. If I hadn't had practice and by now guess what you want to tell me, I would have split my head, like the last time when instead of Caterina [Catherine] she wrote catena [chain]. I don't want the one who writes to be offended by saying this, but to do the best she can.

15.   *October 10, 1937*

Dearest sister,

I'm very happy about the news Mama gave me about you and the children, but she tells me that your husband and Salvatore are the same as ever. We need to have patience and pray a lot. The Lord will surely in the end hear us.

I thank you for the haste with which you sent me the photograph of Caterina when she made her First Communion. I want you to know that my religious profession will be on the 31st and I invite you to take part in my celebration united in prayer together with the children. I'm certain that you will all go to Communion and I especially ask to remember me to the little ones who pray so much for me because Jesus loves children so much and listens to them.

16.   *Grottaferrata, October 10, 1937*

Dearest brother,

I write you these lines to tell you some news. By the Lord's grace I'm fine and hope you are the same. I wrote you for Easter together with Giomaria, but I haven't received a reply. Why? Would you have the kindness to let me know the reason?

As regards myself, I want you to know the 31st of this month I'll make my religious profession. I will be the bride of the Divine King, whose feast is on that day. My dear brother, you know that they give gifts to newlyweds and so I also expect a gift from you.

What gift? you ask me. Here it is, I want you to return to Dorgali on that day to celebrate and that you go to confession and Communion for me. Don't deny me this gift, which is very dear to me and whose fruit will benefit you. I beg you also to persuade Giomaria to go with you. I don't write him since he doesn't know how to read. Don't reply that you aren't in the village because I know that on the feast of All Saints it is a custom for everyone to return home. But if that happens, please do it another day. I'll be happy just the same if you can't go to Dorgali, and you do it at Orosei, for Jesus is as present at Dorgali, Orosei, and Grottaferrata. My brother, overcome the cursed human respect and fear of criticism that hinders you from drawing near to the Lord. Would I be happy and a bride of Jesus today, if I had paid attention to these things? Never. Mama wrote me that you are near Orosei, and therefore if you want to, it will be even easier to go to Mass on Sunday and do what I have told you.

The blessing of the Lord will rest upon you if you will observe His law; but if you despise it, He will abandon you. I await your reply.

18.   *November 2, 1937*

I made my promises in the presence of everyone and I have to fulfill the obligations that I have assumed. I'm sure that all of you are united with me in prayer and so I ask that you pray always that I die, rather than fail in even one of my duties. I received the cards from aunt, uncle, and my godmother who asked pardon for having spoken harsh words to me. Tell her to be at peace, because I don't even remember what she said to me. I received your telegram which gave me so much happiness because of the beautiful words it contained and I thank you very much.

I was very happy to hear that the announcement of my profession was a reason for joy for you too and that you have generously offered the sacrifice to the Lord. I also hope that Salvatore and Giomaria, whom Giovanna greatly recommended that I pray for, have fulfilled their duty and I hope to hear that news from you.

19.   *December 17, 1937*

I do not know if I will still be able to write to you, but anyway I will always remember you who guided my first steps for which I will always be grateful. I wish you a Blessed Christmas. May the Infant Jesus bring gifts of holiness to you and to your people and remove the obstacles you found in your responsibility of which you wrote me.

20.   *December 20, 1937*

I was very happy to hear that on the day of my profession you were united with me in spirit, that you went to Communion and prayed very much for me.

I waited in vain for an answer from Salvatore who seems deaf to what I wrote him. We need to commit ourselves to pray for our men, and Jesus, who can still work miracles, will not fail to give us the desired grace. I have begun to make the fifteen Saturdays to the Blessed Mother for this intention and when they are finished I'll begin again until we obtain the grace.

I received the card from Aunt Grazia that you said shouldn't offend me because of her husband's words. I beg you to tell her for me not to think at all that I'm offended by this, because if she continues to think that way it would make me unhappy, because I know they were not said to offend me, but to test me. But even if I had been offended, it's impossible to harbor resentment when one is in the house of the Lord, since this is something absolutely contrary to our spirit. If I remembered those words it was only to make her understand that if when I left I had been undecided, which for one thing I wasn't, now Jesus has confirmed me more than ever in my vocation.

chapter 8
FOR THE UNITY OF CHRISTIANS

With the advent of Christmas 1937, her third Christmas in the monastery, the curtain falls on the first half of the sacred drama of Sister Maria Gabriella.

From the last two Christmas letters, that of December 17th to Father Meloni and that of December 20th to her mother, we gather two strong points of maximum importance. "I have no illness" she affirms, without imagining how providential and precious her spontaneous testimony will be for us. This is exactly one month before the mysterious events take place. And she adds, with the firmness which distinguishes her: "as for a lack of the spirit of my vocation, I pray rather to die not once but a thousand times if this should happen."

But precisely to indicate that her security is not born from presumption, but from the strength of that abandonment to love in which she has progressed day by day, she concludes with the same steadfastness of faith: "He who has brought me to this point, will sustain me in the future." And three days later, to her Mama: "Jesus has fixed me more than ever in my vocation." Here, I said, the curtain falls.

It will rise again exactly four months later, April 19, 1938, in a radically different situation and scenery. The voice of Sister Maria Gabriella will be heard again, but no longer from the "nest of peace" of her monastery, but from the confusion of a hospital ward; no longer directed to her flesh and blood Mama, but to that one of the spirit, to her Abbess of Grottaferrata, from whom she was almost brutally uprooted Easter Monday, point-blank, in the space of a few hours.

We find ourselves without any letters for four months, from Christmas to Easter, fully conforming to the monastery customs. With the most rigorous and normal Trappistine silence, it hides the most mysterious and dramatic moment of the divine action upon Gabriella in which is irreversibly decided the new course of her spiritual itinerary.

It would seem as if a mysterious director had wanted to respect the classical laws of the ancient tragedies, calling the chorus to speak between the arsis and catharsis of the drama.

Therefore, before restoring the initiative of the discourse to her, it is necessary to stop to analyze the events which filled these four months, allowing the facts and contributing protagonists and witnesses to speak almost exclusively.

As was already pointed out, an ecumenical spirit in the life of the Trappistine Monastery of Grottaferrata, and the Octave of Prayer for the Unity of Christians, inspired by Father Couturier and of which they were strongly conscious, was lived by Mother Maria Pia and her community.

So we see that after Christmas the last two letters of Maria Gabriella are from January 1938, or more precisely, during the 18th to the 25th of January, in the heart of that Octave.

The community of Grotta lives the ecclesial event with its customary thrust, with the full participation and conviction of its religious.

It is the first time that Sister Maria Gabriella lives it as a professed sister, that is after her "little offering."

An old nun, Mother Immaculata Scalvini, had already given herself to the Lord the year before on exactly this occasion with the precise expectation of an offering "for unity." "Can I not offer the little that remains of my life?" she had asked the Abbess with serene simplicity. And the Abbess, with the same simplicity, had told her yes. In little more than a month, on February 25, 1937, the Lord took her, His mature fruit, on tiptoe.

The event was engraved, without a fuss, in the hidden depths of the Novice Gabriella, who made note of the date in her little notebook.

A year later, in the pentecostal atmosphere of community prayer, the new event burst forth without a shadow of an uproar, in the solemn and discreet silence of the Holy Spirit's works. But now, before the witnesses tell us what little there is to know, barely lifting the borders of the divine mystery in the worshipful respect of one who knows that it is the Lord who is acting, it is absolutely necessary to look around in order to discover the premises and background from which the events blossom.

Attitudes of austere asceticism, an oblative spirituality

dominated by the theme of expiation and reparation in union with the divine Victim of Golgotha, these are factors which in the last three centuries dominated a good part of spirituality, especially the French, and were still greatly accepted in the first half of the twentieth century.

These spiritual attitudes and orientations sometimes reached excessive manifestations and were applied in a very offensive manner, almost new dogmas, interpretations, and classifications desecrated and contaminated by Freudian categories.

The school of Olier, of de Berulle and Grignion de Montfort, the penitential message of Paray-le-Monial, of Lourdes, of La Salette and of rue du Bac, then later that of Fatima; the same reparative thrust of the Sanctuary of the Sacred Heart at Montmartre, are many reference points of a determined line of spirituality, subject as every other human expression to immoderation and deviations, but historically very rich in the indisputable fruits of holiness.

Such currents, of a typically French character, were well rooted in the rigid and severe tradition of La Grande Trappe of Abbot de Rancé, and in La Val Sainte of Dom de Lestrange.

It is precisely of such a school and of such a tradition, as we have seen, that the Trappistine monastery of Grottaferrata blossomed.

In this school, in an especially particular manner, was forged the very strong ascetical (sometimes impetuous and exuberant) personality of Mother Maria Pia Gullini. Very Italian by birth and by family, she was the daughter of a state official, but on the ascetical and monastic level passionately attached to the French Trappist mentality of the times. In fact, she was educated and formed in France, as was mentioned, at the Abbey of Laval.

At Laval she imbibed a rigid Trappistine formation, "of the strictest observance." She lived it with uncommon generosity and fidelity, which undoubtedly characterized her government, and of which a few immoderate manifestations appear even in some of the "little flowers," leaving us sometimes holding our breath. At the same time she also had a very strong authoritarian concept of the abbatial function. It was a concept which objectively did not correspond to the balanced guideline left to us by St. Benedict, and which today is no longer acceptable in a renewed post-conciliar mentality, but which at that time was almost customary and univocal.

But even more, Mother Pia had the gift of a precocious intuition of ecumenism, and the good fortune to be able to establish, before its time, a direct relationship of true and profound spiritual fraternity between her community and the Anglican Benedictine Community of Nashdom. She created, in fact, a true and real fraternity, eventually establishing with the Novice Master of that monastery, Dom Benedict Ley, a Catherinian relationship of spiritual motherhood, with the full consent of his Abbot. It is documented by a rich edifying correspondence, providentially surviving the destruction of a great part of the documents of that period.

All of this took place during the Prayer Octave for Unity in 1937 and in a very short time, it increased and blazed in virtue of the humble victim offerings of Mother Immaculata first, and a year later, of Sister Maria Gabriella. In this fascinating progression, we will see a few years later both Roger Schutz and Max Thurian come as pilgrims from Taizé to Grotta, accompanied by Schutz's mother, in order to pray at the tomb of Sister Maria Gabriella. Among other things will follow an intimate spiritual friendship between Mother Pia and Mrs. Schutz which will continue for years. It is documented by some twenty letters, fortunately preserved with other ecumenical mementos of the time in the archives of our Postulator.

In view of these events, is it exact to speak of "ecumenism"?

Personally I believe it is somewhat arbitrary and forced retroactive extension, which would, in part, distort the facts by dressing them in a post-conciliar language and mentality, while we are in a precursory and "prophetic" phase, exactly a quarter of a century before the opening of Vatican II.

Ecumenism, as event and concept, today belongs to the history and culture of the world, and not only to the ecclesial milieu.

The eruptive impetus of the Second Vatican Council and the charismatic zeal of John XXIII and Paul VI brought it forth from the circumscribed areas of special groups study and of prayer and of assiduous, often unappreciated specialized work of a few dedicated people, in order to project it into the full limelight of Christianity in the presence of the entire world.

It is a phenomenon which involves problems of a doctrinal and disciplinary nature and historical research, besides the opening on the psychological and social levels. They are not only basic problems but supremely important ones.

But it is also, and even primarily, a question of openness and adherence to the heavenly Father, "the one true God" (Jn 17:3), of a vital insertion into the mystical body of "him whom the Father has sent, Jesus Christ" (*ibid.*), of listening and of docility to the voice and action of the one Spirit.

And it is, finally, a question which, as courageously affirmed by Vatican II "transcends human powers and gifts. It therefore places its hope entirely in the prayer of Christ for the Church, in the love of the Father for us, and in the Power of the Holy Spirit." (*Unitatis Redintegratio*, #24, Flannery, p. 470)

It is, therefore, above all, a question of grace and the response to grace. Thus, it is a question of individual and ecclesial prayer for the bestowal of a celestial gift which must be invoked from above. . . .

At the time of which we are speaking — 1937 - 1939 — ecumenical activity had dimensions and prospects very much reduced at the level of contacts, while prevailing on every other level and diffusing deeply at the level of "prayer," associated with that of immolation and offering.

When nothing was possible or even foreseen from the "establishment" there happily appeared three shining lights . . . They inflamed hearts with hope *contra spem* [against hope] and the fervor of prayer that moves mountains. With ardent and generous attempts at advancement, they were followed by the amazed attention of a few. They were exposed to criticism, to skepticism, to misunderstanding and to mistrust by many. Surrounded many times by failure and ridicule, they were "sowing in tears" so that others might be able to "reap with joy" (cf. Ps 125:5).

The generous and convinced protagonists who leapt the barrier of separation were Cardinal Manning (1808-1892), Cardinal Newman (1801-1890), and Father Faber (1814-1863); the tormented and reiterated attempts of the Oxford Movement; the resolute initiatives of the United States Episcopalian pastor Lewis Thomas Wattson of Graymoor (1863-1940) who joined the Church of Rome with all his Franciscans of the Atonement in 1909.*

To many it seems utopia.

---

* *Tr.: Mention should also be made of Mother Lurana Mary White (1870-1935),*

The greater part of the initiative came to birth from the midst of the non-Catholic churches themselves. We find the first traces of these generous initiatives among the Anglicans, already in 1838 — exactly a century before Sister Maria Gabriella's offering!

But, rather than an opening, it provoked misunderstandings and mistrust and withdrawals and suspicions.

Meanwhile in the Protestant field, not just Anglican, by means of complex and painful events — which it would be impossible and out of place to summarize here — the initiatives were multiplied and renewed. Even in the Catholic field there was the beginning of a gradual, uninterrupted, even if wary, opening to the problem.

If it is true that the Octave of Prayer for the Unity of Christians originated in the United States in 1907 by Paul Wattson, in collaboration — in England — with the Anglican pastor Spencer Jones (1857-1942), and was launched with unhoped-for success in January 1908 (a year before the passage of Wattson and his followers of the Atonement to the Catholic Church), it is also true that Leo XIII marked his pontificate by repeated gestures for unity. He began by an apostolic letter *gens Anglorum illustris* in April 1895, followed on May 5th by the brief *Provida matris* with which he invited all Catholics to say special prayers in a Novena for the next Pentecost, so that "persevering in prayer with Mary, the mother of Jesus" not to cease "invoking the Almighty Power so that all of the Christian people *una sit fides mentium et pietas actionum*" (AAS XXVII, p. 645). Two years later, the encyclical *Divinum illud munus* made the pentecost novena perpetual.

co-founder of the Franciscans of the Atonement. the timid and courageous Malines Conversations (1921-1925) conducted with so much charity and hope by Cardinal Mercier (1851-1926) and by Lord Halifax (1839-1934); the Benedictine foundation of Amay sur Meuse desired by Piux XI and, after the misfortune of its founder and prior Dom Lambert Beauduin (1873-1960), its transfer in 1939 to Chevetogne; the vicissitudes and vital ferment of the Anglican community of Benedictine nuns at Caldey; the ardent and doctrinal apostolate for the "universal prayer for Christian unity" developed by the writings and meetings of Dom Paul Couturier (1881-1953) a priest of Lyons and a Benedictine Oblate of Amay; these are all names, dates, and events which today are too hurriedly and cleverly put aside. There have been ample documented histories and biographies, by even great authors published about each of the personages, groups, and movements mentioned. But an authentic and courageous history of ecumenism has not yet been written.

It is interesting to point out that while the novena proposed by Leo XIII was placed at the time of Pentecost, it was actually Wattson and Jones who wanted the Prayer Octave to begin on January 18th, the feast of the Roman Chair of St. Peter, and conclude on January 25th, the feast of the conversion of the Apostle Paul. These dates today are in full force with the truly ecumenical support and cooperation of all the Christian confessions.

The strength of these prayer movements was the necessity to respond to the gospel injunction *unum sint*, the desire to remove the *intolerable scandal* of the often mutually disruptive and aggressive divisions; and the painful rivalry especially in missionary lands. It was a truly charismatic movement, of an unshakable faith in the ecclesial presence of the Holy Spirit and the power of His vivifying and unifying action above the divisive pettiness of people.

The word of order for these "fanatics of unity" was the gospel precept of *oportet orare*, accepted and consistently applied until *numquam deficere*.

I cannot help but stop a moment before concluding this rapid and incomplete review on the already mentioned community of Caldey, not only because it has its place, humble but important, in the complex and very erratic events of the journey toward Christian unity, but also because it helps us to return to that January 1938 to the Monastery of the Trappistines of Grottaferrata.

Briefly, it concerns a Benedictine community founded in the heart of the Anglican Church between the last years of the 1800s and the beginning of the 1900s, around the eminent figure of Dom Aelred Carlyle with the powerful support of Lord Halifax and the full approval of Dr. Temple, Archbishop of Canterbury and Primate of the Anglican Church, who in 1902 confirmed the election of Dom Aelred as Abbot. In 1906 the community was officially installed on the Island of Caldey. Situated along the southern coast of Wales, it was expressly acquired by Anglican benefactors and they completely adopted the Benedictine rules, customs, and liturgy, with choral prayer in Latin and Gregorian chant. It was precisely the conscious fidelity to the Benedictine spirit which quickly matured the spiritual crisis of the community which was more and more attracted towards unity with the Church of Rome.

In the course of a few years the crisis irresistibly reached a solution, and was confronted by the monks, with mutual respectful charity in two different formulations.

The principal group, strictly bound to Abbot Aelred opted formally for the Catholic Church, in which they were officially received on March 5, 1913 by the diocesan Ordinary, Msgr. Mostyn, Bishop of Menevia (Wrexham), in the presence of the two great abbots Dom Butler and Dom Marmion. Only in 1928 did these monks abandon the island and transfer to Prinknash in Gloucester. In 1933 they were incorporated into the Subiaco Benedictine Congregation of which even today they constitute one of the most flourishing abbeys. Eventually the community found itself in serious economic difficulties when confronting the first benefactors of the Island of Caldey. Through the desire and personal interest of Piux XI, it was acquired by the Trappist Abbey of Scourmont in Belgium, and in 1928 a community of twenty-three monks was transferred there. From then until today a large part of the Trappist Abbey of Caldey has been formed by elements coming from Anglicanism, and it has a predominantly cosmopolitan structure.

The other part of the Caldey Anglican community, closer to the spirit and mentality of Lord Halifax, wanted to remain in the womb of the Anglican Church, and so remained deeply committed to the original unionist aspirations. Through the initiative of Lord Halifax and under the enlightened guidance of Dom Denys Prideaux, who would become the first abbot, these monks left Caldey in 1914 to take root in the ancient abbey of Pershore near the county of Worcester. In 1926 Dom Prideaux transferred the monastery to its present site of Nashdom, in the county of Buckingham about thirty-five miles from London not far from Windsor Castle. The second abbot of Nashdom, Dom Martin Collet, succeeded Dom Denys in 1935. In full sympathy with his predecessor and with the Novice Master, Dom Benedict Ley, he became one of the most active workers for the union in the bosom of the Anglican Church. He established an admirable bond of friendship and fraternity between Nashdom and Father Couturier, in intimate communion of aspirations and prayer.

Now, it is precisely with the Nashdom community and through the agency of Father Couturier, that Mother Pia established in 1937 the first ecumenical bridge by becoming very involved in the movement of prayer for unity.

At this point, the reader will excuse me for a long digression. I yield the work to Dom Benedict Ley for him to take up the line of discussion, and together with Mother Pia and Father Couturier they return us to Sister Maria Gabriella in the serious and solemn hour of her silent offering for the unity of Christians.

Nashdom Abbey, July 15, 1938

Very Rev. Mother Abbess,

My dear friend, Rev. Couturier of Lyons, allowed me the privilege of reading your letter of December 1937 in which you recount the magnificent offering and death of Mother Immaculata.

Please permit me to tell you how profoundly moved I was by all that you wrote to the reverend priest.

I am an Anglican priest, a member of the Benedictine community established in the Church of England. Among the principal commitments of the community is that of working for the reunion of the Anglicans with the Roman Catholic Church. Therefore you can understand how the immense charity of Mother Immaculata struck me to the very depths of my heart.

The visible acceptance of her offering on the part of the good God is for your separated brethren of England a most valid encouragement to persevere in their labor, often misunderstood and ridiculed, in order to return their Anglican brothers to the fold of Peter.

Dom Benedict Ley

Grottaferrata, July 18, 1938

Most Reverend Father,

Our dear Mother Immaculata left us the fragrance of example and memories. This year, a young professed Choir Sister, barely twenty-four years old, asked to make the same offering. As last year, I had read the invitation of your friend Father Couturier in Chapter. Then I gave her permission, almost forgetting the whole thing.

Now the Sister is in the infirmary, afflicted with pulmonary tuberculosis. She was among the more healthy, without anyone in her family having had the same disease.

M. Maria Pia

Providentially it has been possible to trace the text of Father Couturier's "invitation" for the Octave of Prayer for January 1938. He entitled it: "The Universal Prayer of Christians for Christian Unity." In conclusion, I present the last paragraphs, the same which Mother Pia read in Chapter and which produced a decisive echo in the heart and being of Sister Maria Gabriella.

Without voluntarily closing our eyes to the differences in order to dissolve them in a destructive syncretism of some kind of true faith, we will seek above all to bring out what draws us together. Thus the prospects of convergence will come to light in which will appear the necessity to deny everything that is negative and to re-evaluate our respective dogmatic approaches.

Will it happen that the intellectual will eclipse the spiritual consequences? Certainly not. Prayer will remain the illuminating and living center, rich with a splendid radiance, universality and a visible simultaneousness towards broken Christianity in order to transcend it during these days of January 18-25, or in the following days, on the paths to unity.

The peaceful teaching of unifying research given in each group will rest upon this prayer without introducing a multiplicity of details. Demonstrating the complexity of the problem, we will throw ourselves on our knees in the Heart of Christ in order to repeat together in an act of single and ecumenical love: Grant, O Lord, that unity which You asked for all those who love You. *Congregavit nos in unum Christi amor.*

Will the day come in which the successor of Peter *Vicarius Christi*, the Archbishop of Canterbury, the ecumenical Patriarch of Constantinople, the Patriarchs and Synods of all the autocephalous Orthodox groups, the Protestant Synods and the northern Lutheran bishops, will present to their respective faithful an impassioned invitation to much prayer independent of how agreeable in order to obtain from Christ the great reunion of all Christians?

Intentionally passing over in silence the past which everyone knows, these prayers before God would be like a single cry repeated by everyone together simultaneously, even though separated in their own churches and temples. The gospel prayer of Christ (cf. Jn 17), mounted like a precious stone in the proper rite of each group, would be the most beautiful spectacle that a broken Christianity could offer to the world.

It would be the dawn of Christian unity, and with it the infinite possibility of the evangelization of the masses of pagans . . . and peace for the world.

A dream? An illusion? A simple anticipation of a future reality? We only know that everything is possible before God.

Like Incense . . .

In the writings of the Novice Directress Mother Tecla Fontana, who died November 11, 1955 two years before the opening of the canonization process, one reads the following chronology of the holocaust:

The prayer made to Jesus to consume her as a little host for his glory and the salvation of souls must have been heard. During the novitiate she was always afraid of being sent away, and it was a nightmare for her. But when she was professed she said to Jesus: "Now do what you want, if I'm sick, if I die, it doesn't matter. I'm ready for everything."

In January 1938, on the occasion of the Unity Octave, a new letter arrived from Father Couturier. He spoke of a few lives offered for this goal. An Italian Trappistine nun died February 25, 1937, a Japanese Trappistine, a French Protestant pastor . . .

Sister Maria Gabriella was no longer afraid of being sent away. She quickly presented the sacrifice of herself. In her notebook was found written: "I've never been able to see a sacrifice made without wanting to make it also."

In those days Sister Gabriella confided to me what the Lord asked of her: she also wanted to offer her life for Church unity. This was a subject which could not leave me indifferent. I had spent twenty-five years in service, I had and still have many souls dear to me among the [Christians of other Churches]. Even more, I desired to see them enter the sheepfold of the one Good Shepherd. However, experience had taught me that the great means to attain this is prayer and sacrifice. Sister Gabriella left the prayer to me. She wanted to assume the sacrifice. Could I say no? I immediately had the impression that that sacrifice would be accepted and I lost a daughter of such beautiful expectations. But I had committed myself to the glory of God and I did not delay in giving her my consent. However, I told her that she had to talk to Rev. Mother and follow her decision.

Sister Gabriella, therefore, went to Rev. Mother Abbess. She humbly and sweetly knelt before her, begging her to be permitted to offer her life for the Unity of the Church, "Since," she said, "my life isn't worth much, I don't know how to do anything!" Rev. Mother also feared what I had feared and with an intentionally annoyed manner told her: "I will say neither yes, nor no. Talk to the Chaplain and then the Lord will do what he wants."

Sister Maria Gabriella left the discussion radiant with joy. She took the Chaplain's advice and the offering was made.

. . . The symptoms of the disease with which the Lord would immolate her were not slow in making themselves felt. Had not Sister Gabriella said: 'I am ready for everything, even tuberculosis'?

I who knew the change in the situation regretfully heard the observations some made: "What is Sister Gabriella doing? You no longer recognize her . . . She is pale . . . She has a cough . . ." From the beginning the doctor did not know what he was dealing with; but when the trouble was diagnosed, I could no longer follow her day by day. Rev. Mother took care of it.

I remember (and how could I forget it?) the morning Sister Gabriella had to go to the hospital for the X-ray. Neither she nor we would have imagined that she would have to remain at the hospital. That unexpected departure was a painful surprise for Sister Gabriella and for me. The decision was made in a few minutes. Rev. Mother sent the dear Sister to me to change her shoes. She didn't know exactly what was wanted of her. She needed to go, but she thought that she would return before evening.

She came to me, the leaving overwhelmed her, but she did not say a word. She obeyed at any cost. I asked her to take off her slippers, she looked at me without saying a word, and she obeyed. I felt the vibrations of that tormented heart. . . .

We looked at one another again without saying a word, we embraced in silence, and she left.

Neither she nor I knew that that painful separation would continue for forty days. . . .*

---

* *In the canonical Processes there is no mention of the Roman hospital in which Sister Maria Gabriella was admitted, because none of the witnesses were able to furnish the exact information. This should not be surprising if one remembers that her relatives — by her own desire — did not learn of her illness until after she returned to the monastery, and given the strictness of the rules for enclosure existing then. For a long time the Hospital of St. James was spoken of, but research carried out in the archives of that hospital, as well as at the Polyclinic Umberto I, produced negative results.*

The zeal and perseverance of the first vice-postulator for the Cause, Father Pietro Cappio, were finally crowned with success in January 1966, after the closing of the Processes.

He unexpectedly discovered in the archives of the Hospital of St. John, the "clinical chart" of Sagheddu Maria, twenty-four years old, admitted May 3, 1938 in Ward III of the Hospice Umberto I of St. John. This is the date on which she was transferred for sanitarial treatments by the diagnostic department of the same hospital.

From the photocopy of the document, carefully preserved in the archives of the Monastery of Vitorchiano, emerges not only complete harmony with what Sister Gabriella wrote at the beginning of May: " . . . today they will take me to the ward . . . " (cf. Letter 25), but above all, a valuable confirmation, unknowingly provided by the sick person herself, of the coincidence of the first symptoms of the disease with the Octave of Prayer for Christian Unity. In fact, one reads in her medical history: "From January 16, 1938, she began to have cough, weakness, weight-loss, uncontrolled fever. The said symptoms persisting and having sudden pains in her thorax she was examined and found to have pulmonary tuberculosis, for which she asks admittance."

87

chapter 9

THE LITTLE FLOWERS OF MAÙ

III. The Flowers of the Thorn-bush

153. She made her offering after listening to a passage from Dom Couturier read at the Monastery Chapter in January 1938. She communicated her project of offering herself to the Novice Directress. She presented it to Mother Abbess, and after having consulted the Chaplain, she made her offering with his approval. (183)

154. She made the offering of her own life in January. She began to feel sick in February. I heard her cough in the bindery, in a way that I didn't like, and I notified Mother Abbess who told me that other Sisters who sleep with her and work with her had already made the observation. She made her visit the community Doctor, who didn't give it any importance. He said it was a cold. "Don't you see how strong, how robust this girl is?" (652)

155. The doctor who had to see her didn't want to take an X-ray, because he said, "Don't you see her shoulders? Don't you see what a robust girl she is?" (754)

156. Before making the offering she was never sick. She became ill with tuberculosis. I was the first to realize it, and I told the superior. I had noticed Sister Gabriella stopped on the stairs with a bucket of water on the floor and she was leaning against the wall. I made her the sign "Do you feel sick?" She signed that she felt exhausted. I took the bucket and carried it up to the tower. She followed me in order to close the windows. She didn't say anything, and I didn't think any more about it. But then in the morning, when she went to Choir, since she was in the stall in front of me, I noticed that she coughed. I noticed this for two or three days and told Rev. Mother, "Rev. Mother, Sister Gabriella doesn't seem well." "Why? What have you

noticed?" "You haven't seen her in Choir? She has a cough that I don't like. Besides this, a few days ago I met her on the stairs" and I recounted the incident. "What, daughter, you saw her like this?" and she made a gesture of surprise that I didn't understand at the time. "I will call her." (826/827)

157. At first it seemed like a cold; signs of tiredness and then coughing, then pulmonary tuberculosis was discovered. (540)

158. I remember that she was struck with tuberculosis, which was the disease that Maria feared the most when she was at home. She became sick because she asked the Lord for it. (357)

159. I heard Mother Pia say that there was a relationship between the offering and the disease. She had asked prayers for the Unity Octave. Sister Gabriella presented herself asking to be able to offer her own life for this purpose. She replied, "Daughter, I cannot say." She returned again to ask permission and Mother Pia sent her to the Chaplain, Father Philip Viola. After a conversation with the Chaplain, Mother Pia reluctantly granted the permission, because she was certain that the Lord would accept the sacrifice and she did not like to sacrifice a daughter, but she felt inside that the Lord wanted it. I don't know when she felt the first symptoms of the illness. (602)

160. It was during the Octave of Unity. She made it secretly without fanfare; she didn't even leave a written note. (552)

161. She began Lent like the others. Then Mother Abbess dispensed her from the fast, but she continued to take part in all the community exercises, including the work. Gradually one saw that she was deteriorating, she didn't get over that cough. Mother Abbess told me to have her take a snack in the middle of the morning. I prepared it for her and took it to her in the bindery. She told me, "I take it out of obedience, but it is useless." She had a little fever. (653)

162. We were rebinding all the Choir books and Mother Abbess told me to teach her everything well, in such a way that she could take charge of the bindery. We were mounting the books and I realized she was exerting herself, that she had a stubborn cough, and I said to her, "Now, listen, what is this cough?" She didn't pull the screws well any more, and I asked her, "Do you feel sick?" She answered that her shoulder felt bad. I mentioned it to Mother Abbess, and insisted that she see the doctor again. The doctor found a shadow on her lung, studied the X-ray and so sent her to Rome. (653)

163. At the beginning of the illness, out of obedience to Mother Abbess, she made novenas for a healing and got out in the sun. Then when it was realized that the illness was worse, she thought of nothing but her meeting with God. I know because I had permission to visit her. (548)

164. She didn't neglect the medicine. She was very docile. She bore the illness with great patience. She was very convinced that she must die. (541)

165. During the illness she was always content and suffered gladly for the Lord. When I went to the vineyard, I found her sitting in the shade of a plant, working on a little sewing. I made her a sign to ask how she was, and she responded that she was well, that she was happy to do what the Lord wanted. The Monastery did not have special treatments and she endured everything. (753)

166. At the beginning of the illness she was corrected because she hadn't eaten. She replied, "You gave me that sweet . . . " Mother Abbess corrected her severely. She began to cry (I was present) and then went to church. She had not eaten at table because she didn't feel she could. She was very sick. (580)

167. While the disease progressed she continued the community life. It was her turn to clean the novices' dormitory: tired, faint, she stopped at the middle of the spiral staircase to catch her breath, racked by a stubborn cough. When she became aware of my presence she got to her feet. I tried to help her, but with a sweet smile she made me a sign — no. She immediately picked up the heavy water bucket in her right hand, the broom and dust pan in the left, and thanking me with a sign conforming to Cistercian custom, she climbed the stairs. (234)

168. She observed the fasts until the end. When she was in the infirmary she would accept food only by obedience. In the refectory those near her never remembered that she ever made the sign, "I like it, or I don't like it." (841)

169. I can't say what this Sister likes the most, or what would cost her the most. (179)

170. Even when she already coughed and knew that she was sick she got up just the same at two during the night. (167)

171. We understood from her continual exclamation, "How good is the Lord!" (167)

172. She was willing to come to a Monastery chosen by her confessor. She had the consent of her confessor for her offering.

The only time she was insistent was to be released from the hospital. (578)

173. She did not refuse to remain in the hospital. One time Father Abbot went to visit her. He found her with the doctor, and she humbly begged the doctor and Father Abbot to let her return to the Monastery since she wouldn't get any better. The doctor had no difficulty and said, "Take her to the Monastery." This was recounted to me by Father Abbot, "She knew how to plead her cause so well with the doctor, that she convinced him." (657)

174. One day when the Servant of God felt sick, the Novice Directress sent her to bed, telling her to remain until she was called. The Novice Directress forgot to call her, and at evening Sister Gabriella was still in bed. Another Sister and I went to call her. We said to her, "Why did you stay here?" She replied, "Because I was told to stay until I was called." (735)

175. Most obedient with the nurse and superiors. She took a walk ordered by Mother Abbess until she was seen to stagger. To anyone who mentioned that it would have been better to stay in her room to rest, she made a sign that it was an order of her superiors and she wanted to obey. (658)

176. Sick, on her daily walks she unfailingly stopped to pray at the Grotto of Our Lady of Lourdes. (563)

177. She faithfully and generously observed her religious vows, especially the spirit of poverty. I can confirm this because I was in charge of the wardrobe. When she knew that her illness was infectious, she asked for a work veil and scapular in order to save her other clothes for the community. It wasn't done. When she returned to the Monastery, she found the cowls used from profession too beautiful. She wanted a patched and old one which she wore until her death. Before dying she requested to be buried in old clothes, which was done with the approval of Mother Abbess. (Ord. 61)

178. One time she was upset because she broke a thermometer and looked for Rev. Mother to ask for pardon and a penance, believing that it had been against the vow of poverty. (Ord. 541)

179. Her obedience had to be heroic. Mother Abbess had a bit of originality, and sometimes commanded things that were difficult to obey. For example, by order of her superior she took a daily walk until they had to carry her back to the infirmary. It was Thursday, the day for confessions of the sick. At three

o'clock she went down in a terrible condition. She waited her turn, and then arm in arm with another Sister she returned to the infirmary. From then on she no longer went downstairs except to receive the holy oils. (577)

180. Mother Abbess wanted to disinfect the room where Mother Michael and Sister Gabriella were. She closed the door and windows with the two sick ones inside in bed, and those two girls didn't make one complaint. (622)

181. In July she shared a room with another Sister named Mother Michael who was deaf. Mother Michael couldn't stand the least bit of air, while Sister Gabriella would have taken the roof off if she could have in order to get some air. Mother Michael was very vivacious, while Sister Gabriella was very composed, tranquil, recollected, serene. Nevertheless, they were always in agreement in a mutual, edifying understanding. During the winter which was particularly cold that year, the roof leaked and let in air and cold from every part of the room. They had only one small tin container with a few embers in the room, the only source of heat for them. (Ord. 49)

182. Mother Abbess told us in a community meeting that those two girls were sick from two opposite kinds of tuberculosis. Mother Michael needed a closed place, Sister Gabriella needed air. So she gave the order that the only window would be left half closed and half open in such a way both could make a [sacrifice]. (807)

183. One evening for supper she was brought a plate of potatoes and salad. Given her repugnance at that moment and in that period of time for any kind of food, she laughingly told the nurse, "If it were not for the will of God I would throw this in your face." Out of a spirit of mortification and a spirit of religious poverty she didn't waste any food or anything else given to her. She put it in her cabinet and tried to use it up even if it was bad, unless they took it away secretly. (156)

184. I was in the infirmary but for another illness. Sister Gabriella was in a chaise longue and in the afternoon made the Way of the Cross in the hall. She knelt a long time at every station, perhaps to think of Christ's sufferings. I encouraged her to go faster because of her health, but she looked at me with a smile and continued with the same devotion. (15)

185. For fear that her companions might catch the disease she begged them not to approach her bed. She bore her illness with

great patience. She was happy to suffer because she had offered her life to God. (90)

186. She was always happy and very sensitive for fear of spreading the disease. When she used the stairs, she begged the infirmarian to disinfect the part she had touched with alcohol, and even the door knob to her room. Even the last night, she didn't want me to touch her, since I was the Bursar and had contact with everyone. She said, "This illness is my wealth, but I don't want to share it with anyone." (656)

187. She had a great concern for the community: making visits to the church when no one else was there, holding a clean handkerchief over her mouth, always holding the stair railing with a clean handkerchief. She was forbidden to enter the Novitiate. She went in only once, with permission, at the beginning of her illness, in order to destroy all her writings. (542)

188. I waited at Mother Abbess' door and Sister Gabriella came to the door with a letter. When my turn came to go I thought that Sister Gabriella would take advantage of the open door to go in at least to ask a blessing or greet the Superior. Instead she respected the prohibition, put her letter in the box and left. (542)

189. I noticed that she was very obedient. She no longer entered Rev. Mother's room; she no longer entered the Novitiate; a daily walk, even with a fever of 104; to go downstairs every Thursday for confession until she was no longer able to stand; to be as careful as possible; not even to touch any book of the community, but only the few books she had for her own use; to accept smilingly the window half open. (545)

190. She endured the disease patiently. She gave me the impression of a soul who knows how to encounter death. She often went to make a visit, and manifested tranquillity, joy, and peace. She didn't need anything. Mother Abbess and the nurse were very strict about mortification, and she always accepted everything without a complaint or without looking for special foods. She suffered greatly from the cold, because there was no heating. (654/655)

191. She went remarkably unobserved. She exercised great discretion even in the conferences with her Superiors. She had great docility. (882)

192. Once I asked Father Meloni, who had been at Grottaferrata, for news about Sister Maria Gabriella and he recounted to

me that, contrary to what he imagined, when Sister Maria Gabriella heard that her first spiritual director had come to greet her, she—or better her attitude—was very indifferent and she waited until the Superior told her to go and greet him. (Ord. 415)

193. During her illness she demonstrated a heroic fortitude. The last days were a revelation for everyone. She didn't complain, on the contrary, the more she suffered, the more she tried to smile. (670)

194. During the confinement in the Monastery, when Mother Michael was still in the infirmary, Rev. Mother said, "It seems like an oratory up there, she is always praying." (789)

195. At the beginning she prayed for a healing by command of the Superior. She accepted the fact that she was going to die, and even awaited it. She was devout and prayed with ever greater fervor. She did her reading despite having a fever of 104. (583)

chapter 10
"UPON THE NAKED CROSS"

Rome, April 19, 1938

Rev. Mother,

I am writing these words to tell you the news. Yesterday, a little before noon, that is immediately after my visit to the admissions office, they brought me here to a hospital ward. The doctor has visited me twice. He has told me nothing but to eat and to eat well. The X-rays will be tomorrow. As soon as I got out of the car, I no longer saw the young lady or Sister Serafina and I don't know where they are.

After the first visit to the office, while I still had my undershirt and cap, I was given a gown and told to go with two nurses who were leaving. I thought I would go to another room and I followed them, but I had to cross two or three streets dressed like that. Rev. Mother, I didn't see anything, but imagine my confusion and my pain seeing myself exposed in that way to the gaze of everyone. When I reached the bed that was assigned to me, raising my head I saw a large crucifix in front of me. I stared at it and seeing that my Jesus was naked and that he was exposed to the public out of love for me, I thought that my sacrifice was nothing in comparison to his.

My habit remained at the entrance and they haven't returned it to me, so I am here with a white hospital gown like the others and with my cap on my head. If you could send me a white veil, they told me that I would be able to wear it; and also a lighter T-shirt, because the one I'm wearing is very heavy and it makes me perspire. Thank you. I hope to return after the X-rays. I commend myself to you for this and I have confidence in your prayers. I asked the doctor if he would send me back to the monastery and he answered that he would decide after the X-rays. If, unfortunately, he doesn't send me back, I will let you know as soon as they tell me.

As regards my soul, Rev. Mother, I am like a fish out of water. I am in a large room full of people. Most of them are young people, who cry, yell, and make an infernal uproar and there's no way to be recollected for a moment. As soon as I arrived, they came over to me and wanted me to shout and make noise like them. Now, startled out of my solitude and finding myself in the midst of this world of hubbub, I feel all the greatness of my sacrifice. Even at night coughing is heard to the right and to the left; some complain, others talk, and so it goes.

Now and then, when I think of my monastery and especially at night, the tears fall from my eyes and I can say nothing but these words: "My God, your glory." And so I put myself in peace again. Pray very much for me because I have such a great need.

The Sisters do not see each other except for the distribution of meals. One of them accompanied me for the visit. I asked another one for paper and necessary things for writing. I don't know if she remembered, because she didn't bring me anything. I borrowed everything from one of my neighbors and so please send me paper and a few stamps. I am here doing nothing, having to speak when I would want to be silent and answering the many questions they ask me so as not to be discourteous. Others tell me that they have been here for one month, or two, three, ten months. As for me I believe that I will get worse (instead of getting better) if I have to stay here because everyone is coughing and there isn't enough air. There is a little balcony. I don't go out on it though, because it's above the street and I don't have my veil. I commend myself again to your prayers.

I greet you. United with you in the Sacred Heart of Jesus. Greet the Novice Directress and all the others for me. I will pray for you at Holy Communion.

Sister Gabriella

Sunday, April 24, 1938

Dearest Rev. Mother,

I promised to write to you about the results of the X-rays. They took place Thursday, but the result was only given to me yesterday. I don't understand anything. But if you want to consult the monastery doctor, here is the text: "Radiological examination: Condensation of the entire right superior lobe with the central hyperluminous zone surrounded by smaller areas. Strengthening of the pulmonary design at the bottom."

They won't let me leave. In fact, yesterday they told me I would be here for a short time; today, that I will be here for longer. I cried so much that I can't cry any more. I try to distract myself from this thought and to calm myself, but I don't succeed. My heart is broken and without special help from heaven my cross has become so heavy that I can no longer bear it.

They give me injections every morning and every two days one in the arm. Today they did a pneumothorax on me. It is an injection between the ribs under the armpit. They introduced air into the lungs with a machine. Since this morning it has been painful and I still feel it this evening. Please excuse my writing for I am in bed. They told me not to move, because it could injure me. They introduced 400cc. of air.

I find myself in a hospital where there are not only physical miseries, but also spiritual ones.

I hear things said that I could never stand when I was in the world. Imagine what effect they have on me now. Sometimes I stop up my ears and cover my face, but I can't always do it. This life is a torment for me. Fortunately, a Sister accompanied me for the visit and to have the pneumothorax for which I feel so much repugnance.

Do what the Lord inspires you, but for the love of God, do everything possible so I can return soon to the monastery, because I'm convinced that the doctors exaggerate the importance of my illness. I am sending you the letter I wrote for Mama, because if I send it from here, she would notice the postmark. Don't tell her anything about my illness, otherwise at Dorgali they would say that everyone who enters the convent gets tuberculosis.

If I have to stay here for a long time, I beg you to send me, when you have an opportunity, some work to do, a pair of stockings, a veil, a headband to change, a rosary because I left the one I had in my habit, and a piece of soap to wash my laundry.

I thank you very much for everything that you have written and sent to me. Yesterday and the day before yesterday Father Abbot came to visit me. Pray for me since I have such a need. Sometimes I ask if the Lord has abandoned me; other times I think that He tests those He loves; still other times it seems impossible that God can be glorified by this life. I always end by abandoning myself to the divine will. I greet you with all my heart and ask you to bless me.

Forever your daughter,
S. M. Gabriella

April 21, 1938

Dearest Mama,

I received your two letters and your postcard and I thank you very much. Excuse me and forgive me since I haven't been able to write to you before now. It is certainly not because of indifference or wickedness, but for not being able to. I hope that you all had a good Easter and best wishes to rise with the Lord to an ever holier life. As for me I can't do anything but always bless God for having welcomed me to His house where He overwhelms me with His loving care. Pray for me that I may always glorify the Lord in the fulfillment of His divine will in whatever form it manifests itself.

24.   *April 27 or 28, 1938*

I thank you for your letter and for the prayers that you and the others say for me. I feel their effect because these days I'm a little more peaceful. Everything seems easy when we are in peace; but when the Lord tests us, we become aware of our weakness. I have offered myself entirely to Jesus and I don't take back a word. I am weak, it is true, but the Lord who knows my frailty and the cause of my suffering, will forgive me and I feel convinced of this.

I received the rosaries and holy cards that you sent me and I thank you with all my heart. All of my companions in the ward came around and in an instant the rosaries and holy cards disappeared, because each one wanted a souvenir of the "little sister," as they call me. They lack a little seriousness, but in general they are all good-hearted and like me. They would like to see me always laugh and joke with them; but I refrain, because it's not my way.

After I distributed the rosaries, a Sister saw the one with the dark beads which she liked very much. She asked me if we sell them. She is the Sister who accompanies me for the visits and pneumothorax. And so I ask you to send me one for her, if you think it's all right. Forgive me! I realize I'm being demanding. They let me keep the guimpe you sent me.

As far as the treatment I don't know what to tell you. They did the pneumothorax last Sunday and Tuesday. I have to have it again the 29th. If I cried, it was certainly not without reason, because I know that it is a fairly long treatment and that it often causes many complications. I don't have any fever or expectoration. The doctor would like me to be able to expectorate, but I can't do it for anything. I also asked the Sisters to give me the "cachet" to expectorate, but so far they haven't given it to me.

Rev. Mother, I wish you a happy feast and all that your heart desires. I cannot do anything for you; but I offer my prayers, my Communions, and my sacrifices to the Lord for your intention, asking Him to sanctify you always more. He has not permitted this year that I take part in your feast. *Fiat.*

I do everything that I am told and I eat a lot. I will get better, if the Lord wills it, otherwise may His will be done. May we meet again this day in the Heart of Jesus.

25.   *May 3, 1938*

Yesterday the good Chaplain came to see me and brought me your dear letter. I thank you very much for the concern you have for me and I ask you to thank all the people who are concerned about me. The Lord will reward everyone very greatly in heaven.

I regretted very much having caused you sorrow by my letter. I will not waste time excusing myself; but I ask your pardon with all my heart.

Last Sunday, as I told Father, I had a sputum test and it was found positive. I had focused all my hope on this examination and you understand then the pain this news has caused me.

The first day I suffered a great deal. Then, last evening, I felt a great strength infused into my heart and I was completely resigned to the will of God, accepting the suffering for His glory and not to put my Sisters in danger.

I assure you that my sacrifice is totally complete, since from dawn until night I do nothing but renounce my will in everything and for everything, my aspirations, my desires, and everything that is in me – holy or defective.

Before, there was no way to yield my heart. Now I have truly understood that the glory of God and being a victim does not consist in doing great things, but in the total sacrifice of my own ego. Pray for me, that I may understand more and more the great gift of the cross and profit from it from now on for myself and for all the others.

I feel that now you love me more and that also the love in my heart for you increases. I have suffered a lot about this even from the devil, who has tempted me to judge my superiors without mercy because they leave me here and some people blame them for this. I certainly did not hesitate to get rid of these temptations and I assure you that I succeeded. I tell you this with childlike simplicity and if I could show you my heart like an open book, you would be happy to see it.

The Lord keeps me upon the naked Cross and I have no other consolation but to know that I suffer in order to fulfill the divine will in a spirit of obedience.

It seems to me at times that I've lost my head. Although I begin the rosary, I say the Chaplet of Mercy; I begin this and find myself in the one for the dead, and so on. So I say with the Psalmist: "I have become like a beast of burden, but I am still with you."

I announce to you that today they took me to the ward where I found Sister Serafina; but I don't know yet if they will put me with her. I didn't want to go because Rev. Father Abbot and the Chaplain had told me that I would have to go somewhere else and that this change wasn't necessary, but the order came and I could do nothing but submit. As you see, the Lord doesn't even give you for a moment the consolation of my return and I don't even know if he will give me the grace to return to the monastery.

Please send me, if it's all right, at least the Breviary since you haven't sent me any work; thus, saying the Office, I'll pass the time in a holier way. I don't need anything else now. If I am transferred elsewhere, I will let you know what happens to me.

Rev. Mother, you have asked me to pray for you during these days. You can rest assured that I do that, because my only consolation is to pray as well as I can.

I was not able to finish this letter in the common room and I'm doing it in the ward of the sanatorium.

I was in a little room with a Franciscan religious who seems very good to me. It is much better here than in the common ward and I thank the Lord. I don't know if they will move me again, but Rev. Mother, as the Lord gives you the grace to see farther than I can, do what you judge best.

I feel a great peace gradually entering within me, certainly the fruit of resignation. . . .

Tomorrow and the day after tomorrow I will offer my day for you, praying that the Lord will bless you and sanctify you more and more, so that you can sanctify the others.

I commend myself to your prayers in which I place all my hope.

Bless me . . . The pages that you sent me have been good for those to whom I read them in the public ward. I hope the effects last!

26.   *May 10, 1938*

Yesterday I received your package and your letter and I thank you for everything. I learned of your decision about my return. I know that you are doing everything for my greater good, but I can't hide from you that this has been very painful for me. If you had told me this eight days ago I would not have felt it so much. As for the treatment, I was so resigned that I wouldn't have made a case of it. But now since the Chaplain had told me and still repeated on Saturday that I would be able to return to the monastery this week, I was greatly overjoyed. For this reason, the blow was terribly hard for me, also because I am in a state of great physical weakness.

The wound (moral) was reopened and bleeding again as at the beginning, and made a deep grove in my heart. Patience! The Lord also had this trial to add to the others that followed, so I am sure I will not remain alone. If He wishes, after the first painful moment, everything will be back in its place as before, and His will will be accomplished.

When I left you, Rev. Mother, you told me that if I had to stay it would be a few weeks at the most; but look, a month has passed and who knows how long I will still have to remain. I hope at least that you are not planning to leave me outside too long.

Now that I find myself in the midst of the world again, I feel more than ever the greatness of the gift of a vocation, above all for our life and how much we need to profit by it. Pray for me. When one is accustomed to live the Trappistine spirit, one needs great resignation and a great faith in order to endure a life to the contrary and full of moral humiliations. For consecrated souls it is very painful to be at the mercy of everyone. The doctor is full of concern for me; but that doesn't take away any of my aversion. I am always afraid of losing my religious spirit if I stay here; so I don't leave my room except to go to church. Someone told me that I was too reserved, that I should amuse myself being outside the monastery. I let them talk and feel that if I did that, my spirit would rebel instead, and I would feel worse.

Nothing can give me relief, except the thought of doing God's will and obeying my Superiors. As far as the Religious who is with me, she's also inclined toward solitude. Sometimes our ideas don't agree, but we get along fine just the same. . . . She is absolutely against my departure, saying that if it was the will of my Superiors I would have to do it; but that I shouldn't desire to return to the monastery without having finished the treatment, because I couldn't have the injections there and the special meals as in the hospital. To all of this I reply that I would be much happier to live closed in a well at the monastery, than live here with all the treatments and desirable conveniences.

We go to bed at 9:00 P.M., but for eight days I woke up at 1:00 A.M. or 2:00 A.M.. The pain in my throat and the coughing make me short of breath and keep me from sleeping. During the day I go to bed, but I don't sleep. For two or three days the food disgusts me and I also have a fever.

Forever your daughter who desires nothing but to return to your arms.

The *Imitation of Christ* offered me Chapter 37 of Book III.

27.   *May 22, 1938*

For some time I have been persuaded to be nothing but a pygmy in the way of the spirit, because I let myself be carried by every wind that blows. My soul is lost here, because it doesn't have its Mama (Abbess) and not a friend to whom it can ask advice when it feels the need. It seems to me that the Lord doesn't want me to have human consolations.

When they leave me in peace, I am resigned thinking of the Lord, of His will, forcing myself to overcome the contrary temptations. But if someone, thinking to do me good, comes near me to say something of relief or comfort, my heart bleeds and my eyes cry. Although I experience embarrassment saying it, how can I hide it?

I would like to be strong, strong like iron, and on the contrary, I feel weak like a piece of straw. It is also a trial from the Lord that these thoughts, which I would like to get rid of, keep returning to me insistently.

Yesterday Rev. Father Abbot came. He had talked with the doctor. He said that it was impossible to reduce the treatment to intervals of fifteen days, but within a month it would be reduced to intervals of eight days, then, after seven or eight months, to intervals of fifteen days. I don't pretend that you would take me back since the treatment has to be done every five or six days; but I hope, in any case, that you will not leave me here for seven or eight months.

Often I am also disturbed by the idea that the community has to spend seven dollars a day, as I heard. The Lord who sees all and knows all, will think of this too, so the community doesn't have to suffer for my fault. My Mama, pray very much for me that I won't lose my religious spirit. I have a great fear, my greatest fear, because I feel so weak and capable of falling at every moment. The Lord will help me, because He never abandons those who put all their trust in Him; but I also expect the help of your prayers. The fever had ceased for two or three days; but it returned yesterday evening and this evening. I still have five degrees above normal. I think it's a result of the treatment. I realize now that the distaste with the food comes with the fever.

These rose petals were blessed and distributed at the Mass of Saint Rita. If you want to keep them, disinfect them, because I took them with my hands.

Grottaferrata, June 23, 1938

My good woman,

The Lord has honored and favored you greatly by asking your daughter to be His bride, even now hurrying to the wedding feast.

Dear and good woman, I'll explain. Sister Maria Gabriella, who has always enjoyed excellent health, began to grow pale after a cold, but the doctor said that it was nothing. But that change in color made me reflect and I bade him come again. The doctor found a little catarrh and said it seemed to be unimportant, but to be safer he wanted X-rays. She was accompanied by the Sisters to visit the hospital and doctors, who were of the same opinion as our doctor. However, the X-ray showed a light shadow on the right lung. It was decided to care for her immediately with pneumothorax at a sanatorium. The doctors assured complete and immediate healing. Instead the pneumothorax caused the opposite result, as often happens unfortunately. Since she pleaded to return, she was received back. But there immediately occurred a great and serious change.

It was great suffering for me because your daughter is among the best and I love her very much for her great virtue.

However, knowing that Sister Maria Gabriella had offered herself to the Lord for one of the noblest causes, to speed the union between the separated Churches, I understood that the Lord had accepted the offering.

She told me: "From that day that I offered myself I have not been well." That was at the end of January, but we realized it only in April, otherwise she would have been dispensed from the Lenten fast as she was a little pale as I just mentioned.

Good lady, I know what suffering I am causing you by saying this. I know it because of the pain I experience. But with the eyes of faith see that your daughter is already prepared for the heavenly and divine wedding feast, and cry like a mother cries when a bridegroom asks for her daughter and takes her to his town. They are tears, but I would say of joy thinking of the happiness of your daughter.

Now I assure you that Sister Maria Gabriella is happy, calm, serene, profoundly content. The doctor says, "Perhaps she can recover." But I don't believe it. A strong constitution does not matter if God calls. We have forced her to eat as much as she could. But now she cannot take meat any longer, nor cheese, nor bread. She drinks a lot of milk and also takes four eggs, but everything in order to obey, and also fruit; but she has no appetite.

Dear and good lady, I wanted to let you know, although your daughter did not want to make you suffer. However, do not grieve, like those who have no faith. Your daughter is an excellent religious. I would venture to say now that I see with what sentiments she suffers—I would dare to say: She is a holy religious. Her Sisters in the Novitiate envy her admirable dispositions. The disease can still continue for months. How many? It is God's secret.

Remain at peace for nothing is lacking to your daughter and if you write her, do so as a Mama worthy of such a daughter.

With religious respect,
Sister Maria Pia

chapter 11
"STILL TO MY PEOPLE"

22.

April 21, 1938

I was happy with the news that Sister Andrew brought me from you when she came and I thank the Lord. At Christmas you wrote me of the death of Nennedda and Uncle Delussu. I too was a little unhappy, but we must be resigned to God's will and not only be ready for separation of our loved ones, but if the Lord pleases, also to die ourselves since the future is so uncertain. I'm glad you wrote to tell me because I have been able to pray as is my duty. Even more you should write to tell me these things and even if you have a need for prayer, because necessary things are always permitted and you have never written of useless things.

I hope that everyone had a good Easter. May you rise with the Lord to an ever holier life.

I waited in vain for an answer from Salvatore. It seems that he has arranged for everything and doesn't answer any more. I don't know if he made his Easter duty, but I hope you did everything possible to persuade him. I always pray to the Lord so that He touches the hearts of our men who seem not to want to bend their wills to this great duty. You pray too, because prayer subdues God's arm and moves the divine Heart to compassion. If prayer is not enough I too would want the Lord to make me suffer in order to obtain this grace.

My Easter greeting is that the Lord fill you with graces and blessings according to the desires of your heart.

I embrace you and greet everyone in the Heart of Jesus.

Greetings to relatives and friends. With greetings to you again I beg you to bless me.

I was very happy to hear your letter of reply to Rev. Mother.

In fact, I was convinced that your heart would not deny this ultimate sacrifice. I know that nature wants relief and that one feels the need to cry. But after the first moment is passed, all is cast into the Heart of Jesus, which like a burning furnace consumes everything. As regards my health I don't want to deceive you with a false hope of healing. The treatment that I had at the sanatorium instead of making me well, speeded up the disease and so, since I've returned, I am almost always worse. I don't want you to be worried and pray for my recovery, but pray that the Lord will do with me what is for His greater glory.

Be happy too, my Mother, and thank the Lord for this great grace that He has given you and me. The Lord took this little flower from your house and transplanted it in the cloister and now He wants to carry it to the heavenly garden. Be happy and content, my Mother and all the family. As I am happy, so I want you to be. I certainly cannot forget you because I would be failing in my duty. When the news of my passing arrives don't do the foolishness that they do in town of shutting yourself up and weeping a lot, but bless and thank the Lord and the day after go to Communion and say a prayer for me.

When I am in heaven, I will intercede for you, and the Lord who is so good will console you in your sorrow and shower blessings upon you.

Do not think that I am not being cared for, on the contrary they are taking very good care of me. Rev. Mother is so good. She doesn't spare herself any effort and seeks every possible means to bring me relief. She comes to the infirmary to visit me every day. That is a great sacrifice for her because we are more than fifty and she has to attend to everyone. No motherly heart could surpass her in love and in all the attention she shows. Pray for her because she has a right to your prayers since she sacrifices so much for me.

And now, my Mother, I ask pardon for all my failings and all my offenses while I was with you and I also ask pardon of the entire family and aunt. From you, my Mother, I await your blessing. I recommend myself to everyone's prayers in order to be able to suffer in a holy way all the sufferings that the Lord will be pleased to send me.

Everyone, resign yourselves and rejoice in the Lord. Don't let yourselves be overcome by sorrow; but be happy as I said, and bless God for all that He does.

I greet you together with all the family, and greet all the relatives for me. I embrace you in the Heart of Jesus.

Your daughter,
Sister Maria Gabriella

Note: The letter was accompanied by this note to the Rev. Mother:

I did not write the address because my hand does what it wants to. I filled the pages so as to please Mama, but perhaps not two words make sense.

29. *July 15, 1938*

Remembering you always and the good you have done for me I believed it my duty to write to you a last word of thanks and to express my gratitude again. Please do not mind the writing because my hand goes its own way. The Lord permitting it, I have contracted a disease (Rev. Mother will explain to you) which I hope will bring me to the eternal wedding feast.

Therefore I want to express my gratitude to you. Thank you very much, Rev. Father, that you cared for my spirit from its first awakening to true life and guided it along the path that the Lord inspired and that you have always helped my soul. I thank you for having had such concern for my vocation and for having strengthened it from its birth for the trials of life. Oh! My vocation! If my dream comes true, I feel I owe a large part to you, who have also been concerned about my family. If I find myself in this blessed sanctuary, after the Lord I surely owe everything to you. My heart overflows with gratitude, but the words are too miserable to express what I feel in my soul. The Lord who is so good will reward you for all you have done for my poor soul. But if you were the first to work this arid ground, you should be the first to gather the fruits. When I am up there, if the Lord will be pleased to take me, I will intercede for you and the good God will not fail to shower upon you His heavenly blessings.

I hope to be your first spiritual daughter to die as a Sister, and so I commend myself to your prayers that I can be purified and sanctified before the Bridegroom comes.

I hoped, as you promised me, to be able to see you again on this earth, but if this is not possible, we will certainly see one another again in Paradise.

Praying that you accept my best wishes, I ask for your fatherly blessing.

30.   *July 21, 1938*

I received your dear letter the other day and I am happy with your news. Yesterday the cookies that you sent us arrived. Thank you very much. I tasted them and I found that they had the same flavor as when I was at Dorgali. They are very good.

Oh! How beautiful it is to live in the house of the Lord, where there is one heart and one soul.

But I don't want to say that at home I never enjoyed peace and tranquillity, but rather in this regard I can attest that our family was always a model for the neighbors.

I thank you very much, my Mother, for the warm acceptance you have made of the sacrifice. I am happy not only to offer myself, but to be offered also by my dear ones as a victim of holocaust to be consumed, if it pleases God, for the salvation of souls.

My Mother, I understand your suffering and sympathize with you, but think that the greater the sacrifice, so much greater will be the reward that you will receive up above. Do you believe perhaps that I am insensitive to your suffering? Oh no. In reading your letter my heart bled and tears fell from my eyes for your suffering has become mine. I can't understand how there are persons who dare to say that when we become Sisters, we forget our family. Our love is, however, different from before because it is supernaturalized, but for all that it is much stronger than before. How can we forget our dear ones who have given us life, reared us with care and sacrifices, loved us and love us so much? We have made the sacrifice to leave them, but we are well rewarded with the joy of living in the Lord's house.

I have taken a long time to describe these things to you and have not yet told you something that you will certainly like. Last week Mr. and Mrs. Muceli came to visit me. The visit made me very happy because they were so good to me during the trip treating me like their daughter. They were also very happy to see me and in fact told me that I didn't even appear to be sick.

The Lord is so good to cover the signs of the illness with a veil. They told me they would write to Dorgali and they would also send you a note and I hope that they kept their promise. This was also a consolation for me. When I think of the tenderness and delicacy that the Lord uses with me every day in every way, my heart is moved and I am filled with a great joy. My God, I then say, if you treat me with such gentleness on this miserable earth, what will happen when I go to enjoy you above in Paradise? My Mother, my happiness is so great that I cannot compare it to any good or joy of this world.

I am grateful to Maria Mereu and I thank her very much for her prayers, and I will also pray for her. I greet the whole family and embrace you in the Heart of Jesus.

Greet the relatives and friends for me, and especially Madrina Michela.

I embrace you again and am always your daughter.

Sister Maria Gabriella

31. *August 17, 1938*

I received your letter several days ago and I am very pleased with your news. God will surely reward you for the love and resignation with which you have embraced this cross He has sent you.

You are firm in your dispositions of abandonment to the will of God and always bless Him in some way for what He has done in my regard. Forget that I am sick and think only of the Lord, in order to thank Him and bless Him for the graces and gifts He has given me.

I want you to know that at the end of last month Father Meloni came to pay a visit. He was very happy and so was I and the others. This visit brought great joy. You, my Mother, wrote me that if you had been able, you would have hurried to come to see me. It seems that the Lord makes this impossible and so you sacrificed this desire to the Lord. Your crown will be adorned with another very beautiful diamond.

32. *September 22, 1938*

I was glad to hear that you had received my news directly from Father Meloni because in this way you will be more peaceful about me. Now I am better and they give the Lord thanks for that. I am in the same dispositions as before and thank the Lord for what He has done for me. You also always hold to the greatness to which He has called you, because He has given you a great honor in choosing a bride from your family. But not only that, but a chosen bride for the sufferings are nothing other than a sign of divine predilection. I thank and will thank and will bless the Lord forever for what He has done for me and for you; but I feel that I will never be able to thank Him enough.

33.   *December 18, 1938*

In the letter you wrote that Salvatore was recalled, but then you didn't tell me anything in the note and so I don't know if he returned. If he did, tell him I am still awaiting his reply. If he hasn't returned, send me his address. You wrote me that my cousin Paul Monni was sick, but I hope that now he is well. However, when you wrote, you didn't give me news.

I joyfully await the feast of Christmas. I hope to spend it with the Infant Jesus since this year I'm more united in a special way with Him by means of the Cross. I send best wishes to you and all the family that this heavenly Child will bring you joy, peace, and holy happiness. As the angels sing at the holy crib, I hope that they sing around you: Glory to God in the Highest and peace on earth to people of good will.

This Infant God of ours gives us so many lessons that perhaps we will never be able to understand fully. He, the creator God of the universe, humbles Himself to be born in a poor stable, an inn for animals, where He was completely unknown. Look at how we are completely the opposite. We are almost embarrassed to be poor and at certain times we would almost want to hide our poverty, because it seems to humiliate us. We don't realize instead that this is a privilege from the Lord, because it makes us like Him. Who will dare to rebel, thinking of the humiliations and sufferings of the God-Man?

My wish for you and for everyone, my dearest Mother, is that the Divine Infant give you His own virtues from His crib — sweetness, humility, love. May this feast be for you one of holy joy and happiness as it is supposed to be.

I wish everyone a holy New Year full of heavenly blessings conforming to your desires. May the Lord in this new year make you grow more and more in sanctity and in love of Him. I do not desire that you become rich and well-off, but that you are always holier and more abandoned to the will of God and so I always pray to the Lord that He gives you the graces necessary for your vocation. I desire that you want this always for me that I may always be holier and continually grow in the love of the divine Bridegroom, from whom I have received so many graces and favors. Pray for this.

I will be united with you in thought and soul at the crib of the Child Jesus, and through Him I greet and embrace everyone.

34.   *December 19, 1938*

Rev. Father,

I thank you for the visit that you were pleased to make and that did me so much good. I ask pardon for not even saying goodbye before your departure. I didn't know about it, in fact the next day I waited for Mass, but Rev. Mother told me that you had left immediately.

I thank you for taking my news to Mama, and from what she has written me, it did her a lot of good.

35.   *February 1, 1939*

Rev. Father,

Rev. Mother read me part of your letter that you had written to her. I was touched. I feel from your words how the Lord tests you and how much you have to suffer. We have offered ourselves by our consecration and the Lord has honored us by taking us at our word. I am sure that our sufferings will be for the greater glory of God and for the greater benefit of ourselves and for the salvation of souls. My Father, let us raise our spirits and our souls to the Lord and He will console us and He will not abandon us in tribulations. Everything works together for the good of those who love the Lord, says the apostle. Pardon me, Father, if I speak in this way, but your words reveal a little bit of depression and lack of trust and the Lord has inspired me to write you in this way and I have obeyed the inspiration.

I always pray for you and keep you in my heart and I offered my Communion for this today.

I also pray for those two aspirants to our life and I hope that the Lord, if it is for His glory, will do everything.

I ask your pardon for my boldness and ask you for your blessing.

36.   *February 2, 1939*

Rev. Father,

Yesterday I wrote you a note for which at the present I am distressed.

I'm sure I interpreted your words badly and therefore spoke unworthily and with little respect. Since Rev. Mother had to mail another letter, I thought it my duty to write to you again to ask forgiveness.

The words in your letter that struck me the most were that you asked the help of prayers with infinite anguish. They didn't explain what I believe, but I am sure that you wanted to express the infinite anguish which flows from the Heart of Christ to ours when we see Him offended, insulted, abused, and even when we see souls lost, and we want to do everything possible to save them while they throw themselves headlong into the eternal abyss.

The Lord made me understand very well how you, already so accustomed to trials, could not let yourself be defeated by them. I ask your forgiveness and pardon for having spoken so badly and without the respect I owe you.

As you well see, I am still the same. I have a weak head that speaks without reflecting on what it says. I certainly hope that you will pardon this mindless talking and pray for my conversion. I too, will continue my prayers for you.

37.   *Grottaferrata, March 25, 1939*

Dearest Mama,

Even though in our Order we usually don't write during Lent, Rev. Mother wants me to send you this note to give you a little news. The Lord willing, I am still in about the same state as when I wrote to you the last time. I'm still in the infirmary because my health doesn't allow me to work with the others and this disease requires a little separation from the others.

I received your Christmas card and your letter. Thank you very much. When you send picture postcards, don't put more than five words, otherwise there will be a charge. Since more than anything else my Office and work is to pray, I always pray for you and commend you to the Lord that He may help you in all your needs and make you always grow more in holiness. I wish you and all the family and relatives a happy and holy Easter. May it be happy and rich in grace and heavenly blessings for you.

Rise with Christ to a new life. Run with Him in the ways of love and abandonment with greater strength.

chapter 12
THE LITTLE FLOWERS OF MAÙ

IV. The Flowers of the Rock

196. She awaited death. She desired Paradise, but waited for it without hurry. We never saw her depressed when she was sick. She was a strong soul who had no time to think of other things. (566)

197. While before they were in the habit of burying the nuns in the public cemetery, at a certain time they began the practice of burying the Sisters within the boundaries of the Monastery after obtaining permission from the Vatican. Meanwhile, Sister Gabriella was very ill and approaching death, but the expected permission hadn't arrived. At a certain point the authorization was finally granted, and the Abbess told Sister M. Gabriella who, completely happy, exclaimed: "Now I can die peacefully." That was to say that she didn't want to leave the Monastery even dead. (Ord. 241)

198. Sister M. Gabriella came down from the infirmary for the next to the last time for her regular walk ordered by the nurses and Mother Superior. On that day her strength failed and the other Sisters had to help carry her up the stairs to the infirmary. An hour later, at about 3:00 P.M., she left the infirmary again to go down to the chapel in order to go to Confession. She stayed until the last since she was the youngest. I saw her while she was waiting for her turn. She was seated on a low wall in the cloister, bent almost in two. Her face showed a great deal of suffering like one who has made the greatest effort and can do it no longer. (Ord. 52)

199. The last time she came down—it was Good Friday—to receive the Holy Oils in Choir in front of the grille. She was assisted by Sister M. Benedetta, the infirmarian at the time. She was smiling and radiant. One would say like a bride going to the

wedding feast. She asked pardon from all of us for her failings before receiving Extreme Unction. Father Philip administered the sacrament, exhorting her briefly about the offering of her life to the Lord. (Ord. 52)

200. The last time I visited her, the day before she died, Rev. Mother was weaving a crown of fresh flowers and was almost finished. I said, "Look, Sister Gabriella, what a beautiful crown. It's almost finished." She said, "Oh! Yes, let's hope that it will be finished soon." I said, "Courage, it lacks the most precious pearls," and she, "Oh, yes, let's hope that it will be done soon. Oh! How happy I am!" (833)

201. Shortly before Sister Gabriella died, I learned of the vow for the unity of the Church from Mother Pia. She made it in January during the Unity Octave, after having heard that Mother Immaculata had offered her life for unity. She persevered in her decision until the very end. It seemed that she knew death was near. The last night while I was present she was suddenly fearful. She cried out asking Rev. Mother, "I can't go on. What should I do?" She looked at us as if to say, "What do you suggest for me?" The Chaplain said to her, "Passion of Christ, console me." Mother Pia said, "You offer everything for unity, don't you?" She replied, "Yes." During the agony she said to us, "What should I do?" We prayed a little and offered ejaculations to Jesus for unity. She took courage and became calm. It seemed that an ejaculation, a good thought that was suggested to her, had the effect of a sacrament. (659/661)

202. She had a very humble opinion of herself. The last night when Mother Pia showed her an image of the Sacred Heart sent by Dom Benedict Ley, an English Anglican, for her to sign and then return to Dom Benedict, she was very embarrassed, saying, "But what's the use? Why?" She signed it reluctantly. Then she was made to look at it and kiss it, but she was not at all interested in the esteem of that prelate. (671)

203. She was so sure of going to heaven that when I asked her to remember me she replied, "As long as I'm on this earth my head's not much, but when I am in Paradise I'll pray for you and for everyone." (Ord. 524)

204. She was very ill during Holy Week and they expected death from one moment to the next. She too awaited it and often said, "Jesus will take me as the Paschal Lamb." (Ord. 249)

205. She did not make a will because she did not have anything to leave, with the exception of good example. (338)

206. Shortly before dying she told me, "Accept my advice! I tell you this: when Rev. Mother gave me some order I always followed it. And Sister Margaret, if you do the same, you'll find happiness." Regarding her humility, no one knew of her offering, neither her confidants nor her fellow-peasants. (Ord. 528)

207. Almost the entire Community was present, but only a few fit in the small room. (585)

208. There were present: Mother Pia, Sister Benedetta the infirmarian, Sister Adelaide, myself, the Chaplain. At 2:00 A.M., she began to say the Office in her room, and her face was transfixed. She had the expression of a seven- or eight-year-old child, a beautiful smile. She was very quiet after the Office until the end (about 4:00 A.M.). One would have said she no longer suffered. (622)

209. I was right next to the bed. The Servant of God was dressed and she tried to take off the headband in order to breath better. Rev. Mother said to her, "Down, down daughter, put your hands down." She lowered her hands and didn't move any more. She remained alive another three quarters of an hour. (585)

210. She received Communion after the two o'clock Office (at about 4:00 A.M.). Then in the morning, seeing that she was worse, she was brought Viaticum (about 7:00 or 8:00 A.M.). In the late morning she went into a semi-coma. After Vespers she opened her eyes. She had a look of surprise, of joy. She immediately closed her eyes and expired. (674)

211. I saw Sister Gabriella's small devotional book which contained some important dates which she had written. Among these dates was the death of Mother Immaculata who was the first to offer her own life for unity. However, I don't know what happened to the little book. (752)

212. When she had expired, the Sisters had to ring the death toll. We said, "Go ring the bell." The bell sounded for a feast, not a toll. I said to Mother, "Do you hear? They've made a mistake." The two Sisters returned upstairs and I said, "But what have you done? Have you rung for a feast?" The Sisters assured us that they had tolled the bell. The bells at St. Joseph and also at another parish had rung at the same time for a feast. (675)

213. Immediately after the death when Mother Pia asked me,

"What do you think of Sister Gabriella?" I responded, "To me, if that's not holiness, I'll never understand what holiness is." (668)

214. I share the thought of Rev. Mother Pia who one day said to me, "Now Sister Gabriella is a daughter who has run away from home." (591)

215. She had asked her mother: After my death recite the Magnificat and don't make all that fuss as they do in Dorgali. She spent her very last moments in a coma. I don't know what her last words were because when I reached the infirmary she was already in a coma. She left no testament: only a letter to her Mama that was prepared a few days before, to be given to her after her daughter's death. (586)

chapter 13
IN PROFOUND PEACE

28.   *July 6, 1938*

I am happy to be able to suffer something for love of Jesus. My joy becomes greater when I think that the time of the real wedding feast is approaching. As you know the Lord has always favored me with special graces, but now with this illness He has given me one greater than them all. I am completely abandoned into the Lord's hands and I have profited greatly. I feel I love my Bridegroom with all my heart; but I want to love Him even more. I want to love Him, for those who do not love Him, for those who despise Him, for those who offend Him. My desire is nothing but to love.

What joy the day that these bodily miseries disappear and I can go to contemplate the Heavenly Bridegroom face to face! My joy is so great and no one can take it from me. It is greater than that which the rich enjoy in their palaces, for in their enjoyment their hearts may perhaps be dead. There is no greater happiness than to be able to suffer something for love of Jesus and for the salvation of souls.

Grottaferrata, July 9, 1938

Good and dear Mrs. S.,*

I just now received your second letter. For three days I have had a letter from Sister Gabriella without finding the time to send a note with it.

She was a little bit better this week; less fever and she also slept. Perhaps it is her Mama's prayers. But it is not an improvement to trust. She is very calm, content!

---

* *Tr: These letters are from Sister Maria Gabriella, Mother Maria Pia, or the Anglican Dom Benedict Ley, as can be seen from the context. "Mrs. S." refers to Mrs. Sagheddu.*

Remain peaceful Mrs. S., I will keep you informed and, if possible, I will have Sister Gabriella write, even though it costs her great effort. I thank the Lord that her Mama is worthy of her daughter. Pray much for her, that the holocaust may be worthy of God. About the cookies—Sister Gabriella told me she will try to eat some to please you. If you wish, send a pound, not more. We also have dates here, but she has no appetite. Thank God she still takes milk, eggs, and fruit. The Lord allows other special things to be offered, bananas or others, which make her think of the delicacy of Providence.

Recently when I told her that her Sisters in the Novitiate were making a novena, she said, "With all these prayers and these remedies they won't let me die! But I'm happier to go with the Lord. But whatever He wants!"

29. *July 15, 1938*

I will be happy and my happiness is truly great. What joy to be able to suffer something for love of Jesus and for souls. I made a great act of abandonment into the Lord's hands, and my heart and soul are immersed in profound peace, in great happiness.

When I think of the blessed day, when these bodily miseries will fall away and I can go up above to embrace the Heavenly Bridegroom, then my joy and my happiness extends beyond the earth.

July 18, 1938

Very Reverend Father,

"Since the day of my offering I have not spent one day without suffering," she confessed to me much later, when I was suffering greatly and asked where this evil came from. Then I seemed to remember that it was precisely she who begged me in January to let her offer her life for Unity. And when I asked her about it, she gave me that answer.

It is Mother Gabriella—a beautiful daughter, pure, serene as an angel. During the Novitiate she was not disobedient once. Gifted with an uncommon intelligence and an extraordinary memory, she has used it to be "faithful"! Forgetting herself, she has passed silently and unobserved. Only now that the Lord calls her do I realize what a treasure she is.

Easter Monday she was taken to the sanatorium for a simple X-ray. They kept her for forty days trying all their cures. She returned suffering so much that it seemed she'd been sick for two years. The pneumothorax treatment had the opposite effect, as often happens, that is, making the disease progress.

I do not know how many years or months the good God will allow her to live. She longs for the wedding feast. She wrote her Mama a marvelous letter. Very simple and very calm, she seems to actualize completely a phrase of Bernadette: "What concerns me, no longer concerns me." She never complains in the midst of her sufferings. She reached a point of abandoning herself to the good pleasure of God which reveals the action of God Himself in this chosen soul.

I go to see her every evening and I confess to you that this is a joy, a strength, a real spiritual comfort for me. Pray for her and commend her to the prayers of your Sisters. Help her in her preparations for the marriage banquet. I am sure that she will know how to repay your gifts. I hope that she glorifies her Jesus and that He glorifies her next to Himself. You, Rev. Father, are blessed in your good will and in your desires.

30.   *July 21, 1938*

As far as my health these days, I am much better. May the Lord be thanked for everything. I am always happy to do the will of God, whatever it may be, and this is my joy, my happiness, my peace. Rev. Mother is so good and doesn't spare any labor or sacrifice in order to relieve and please me. My Sisters in the Novitiate do nothing but pray because they really want to see me return to them.

The Lord is so good to cover the signs of the disease with a veil.

July 21, 1938

Dear Mrs. S.,
    Thank you very much for the cookies which pleased your

daughter very much. The hoped for improvement truly occurred. She is almost without fever throughout the day. She is eating again and also taking a small piece of bread.

She really feels better in every way. I do not know what to think, except to confide myself to the immense love that God has for us, and to ask only that He fulfill His designs for His greater glory. Sister Maria Gabriella still continues to be calm, serene, happy; always edifying. It is a pleasure to be with her, because one feels that she is always with the Lord. Remain at peace now, dear Mrs. S., I will keep you informed. I thank you very much for the prayers that you say for me. They are real charity.

Sister Maria Pia

Nashdom Abbey - August 6, 1938

I cannot tell you how moved I was by what you told me of Mother Maria Gabriella. I will not fail to pray for her, also asking the others for their prayers. It is a great joy to know something about her. It could be that she is unable to recite her Office, in such case, I could say it in her place. Doing it, I will feel more united to her. . . .

Permit me to send a few words and a little picture to Mother Maria Gabriella, as a little remembrance of my prayers for her intentions.

Benedict Ley

Nashdom Abbey - August 6, 1938

Your charity will permit one of your separated brethren to thank you from the bottom of my heart for the offering you have recently made for Unity.

This greatly resembles the Savior's Passion in which He clearly demonstrated the thirst that the Father has and He has for us. While you unceasingly offer yourself to divine Love — and may this love be fully glorified in you — you will have the joy of knowing that your separated brothers are attracted to the Most Sacred Heart of our Lord, for He said, "As for me, when I shall be lifted up from the earth, I will draw all to myself." From now on while reciting the Office,

I will do it in your name, in union with you; or better, I will seek to offer myself to Christ that His prayer for you may be reproduced in me. He will fill you Reverend Mother, with Himself, so that the divine life of the Most Blessed Trinity which is so rich and splendid, can manifest and glorify itself in you. What a marvelous thing to be called by Him who lives in us and reigns over us!

The Holy Virgin, your Mother and ours, who with Jesus and with you has suffered in our place, remains near you as she remained near the Cross. You can count on Her. Your poor separated brother

Benedict Ley

31. *August 17, 1938*

As far as my health, I thank the Lord that I am a little better, but the disease has taken hold and who knows what the Lord will want to do with me.

I am always content and even if sometimes I suffer, that doesn't hinder me from being in the joy of the Lord.

August 17, 1938

Sister Maria Gabriella remains in a better, or at least in a "not worse," condition. Little fever, not much cough, fairly good appetite, and her soul always in excellent health. In the beginning this almost stopped her from being examined. Now she is happy just the same. Her will is more and more united with that of the Lord.

32. *September 22, 1938*

Now I find I'm better than then [when Father Meloni came] and they are giving thanks to the Lord for that. It seemed for a long time that I would go to Paradise and instead the Lord keeps me in this kind of exile. Surely that means that my crown is not yet finished.

I'm in the same disposition as before, and I thank the Lord for what He's done for me.

Nashdom Abbey - November 6, 1938

Most Rev. Mother Abbess,

My friend Father Couturier of Lyons asked me to write to you to recommend the coming Octave in the Angelican Church to your good prayers.

Frequent and vibrant are my prayers for good Mother Maria Gabriella. I have also asked others to pray. If you think it possible, I would like very much to know her state of health and if she could write me a few lines, I would save them as the word of a person crucified with Jesus.

Humble and religious regards. Assure Mother Maria Gabriella of my prayers. Your poor separated brother

Benedict Ley

November 11, 1938

. . . Mother Maria Gabriella . . . goes on . . . She is an admirable creature, humble, abandoned, generous and very wise . . . wise with wisdom. The infirmarian told me, "When she speaks she is so simple and controlled—not a word too many—that one could write what she says." As far as the illness, it is better, much better; but one cannot trust that bacillus. For now she has no fever, the cough is bearable. She is always content, content to suffer, content with the good God, with her vocation. How her large eyes sparkled when I told her of the offering the Holy Father Pius XI had made of his life!

33.   *December 18, 1938*

I am thanking the Lord that I am much better. Since the month of August the draining of liquid has stopped so that I no longer have fever and the other pains have also diminished. For a long time it seemed that I would go to Paradise and instead it seems that the Lord has decided to prolong my pilgrimage. May He be blessed in all things.

Although I'm better, one should always be prepared for death since in a short time we have had two earthquakes which don't make us safe. Don't fear anything, but pray that if the Lord comes, He finds me prepared.

34. *December 19, 1938*

I thought that by this time I would already be in Paradise and instead it seems that the Lord wants to prolong my pilgrimage on earth. May His divine will always be done in everything.

Living in abandonment I have never had to regret the past and so I am certain of the future. I'm sure that Jesus will do what is for His greater glory and best for my sanctification.

Since August I have had no more fever, and the other things are also better, even though the little daily troubles are not lacking. But what value would there be to being in the infirmary if one had nothing to suffer? Without the battle there is no victory, and so without suffering we cannot expect the crown.

Jesus has chosen me for that privilege of His love, giving me suffering in order to make me more like Himself and I am very happy and thank Him.

I feel that I will never be able to understand sufficiently the love that Jesus shows me in offering me this cross.

Certainly the illness is a little humiliating for nature, which has some moments of struggle, but love and grace soon win and the humiliations of nature become the dearest delights of the soul.

37. *March 25, 1939*

I am almost always in the same condition as when I wrote to you the last time since the Lord wants it this way. I'm still in the infirmary, because my strength doesn't allow me to work with the others, and besides, this illness demands a little bit of separation from others. I lack nothing that a sick person could need; on the contrary, the superiors compete in order to bring me some relief. So I tell you that I'm treated like a queen and not like the miserable person that I am. Don't be sad or grieve for me, because I am always happy and content with everything that the Lord arranges.

I received your Christmas card and your letter. Thank you very much. When you send picture postcards, don't put more than five words, otherwise there will be a charge. Since my Office and work is to pray more than anything else, I pray always for you and recommend you to the Lord that He may help you in all your needs and make you always grow more in holiness. I wish a good and holy Easter to you and all the family and relatives. May it be for you happy and rich in grace and heavenly blessings.

Rise with Christ to a new life and rush forward with Him with greater effort in the ways of love and of abandonment.

Pray for me that Jesus may find me more and more worthy of Him.

I greet and embrace everyone in the Lord.

Your daughter, Sister Maria Gabriella

Grottaferrata, March 29, 1939

Good and dear Mrs. S.,

Your daughter approaches Paradise with an intense desire of soul and the progression of the disease. Calm, peaceful, always content, always ready for sacrifice, always truly more an angel than a creature here below. Do not think that I exaggerate or say that because you are her Mama. It is precisely this way and even more so.

She is surely a blessing for you and the family and she will be even more one when the Lord of heaven and earth will have taken her to reign with Him.

Dear and good Mrs. S., pray for your daughter, that her virtue—dare I say her holiness—(holiness made of joy, humility, abandonment to God) may grow ever more.

Humbly
Sister Maria Pia, OCR

Holy Saturday (April 8, 1939)

Good and dearest Mrs. S.,

A few days ago your daughter said to me: "It came to my mind that perhaps He will take me like a Paschal Lamb." And perhaps it is true. She declines rapidly. We have already given her Extreme Unction last Friday, and today Holy Viaticum. She desired them so much! She has been so happy and is happy. When she says, "How good is the Lord!" and smiles and raises her eyes with her habitual gesture, she is transformed and seems like an angel to me.

Dear Mrs. S., how I would like to satisfy you with a photograph! But we are cloistered, no one can come in, and those who knew a little about photography are no longer able to do it. Make this sacrifice too! She greatly resembles Sister Thérèse of the Child Jesus, with those large eyes of hers that make us think of Paradise. She is calm, serene, content! She takes some cookies with mineral water. We have put orange juice in the water like "soda" and she can take it and smile because it is from her home.

Mrs. S., I am certain that because of your daughter, the Lord will bless you, your home and many others! It can still be prolonged, I do not know exactly. The Lord knows and does everything well. Let us leave it to Him and thank Him.

With affection,
Sister Maria Pia, OCR

38.   *To be delivered after death*

[*written in pencil by a different hand*]

Dearest Mama,

I write you these lines in order to send you my last thought and my last greeting. The divine Bridegroom has renewed the invitation and the longed-for day approaches. I don't say to you the day of death, but the day on which, released from the bonds of this miserable flesh, I will be able finally to pass from this life to the happy and blessed one of heaven. Separation from the body is not a death, but a passage to true life. Rejoice, O my Mother, because up above there will no longer be enclosures and I, even though you won't see me, will be able to come visit you and embrace you so much because I feel my love for you increasing more and more. Be at peace, because from above I will be much more useful to you than I have been here, because from there I will see clearly all your needs and I will be able to intercede more quickly with the Lord. Do not cry and don't make the fuss that they do at Dorgali, because you would make me very unhappy.

I desire rather, that on the same day that you receive the news, all of you go to holy Mass and Communion and so pray for me and thank the Lord so much for the grace He has given me and for the favors He has done in my regard. I hope that Salvatore and my brother-in-law have fulfilled their Easter duty, but if not, I very much encourage them to do it as soon as possible, at least to do it as my last desire. I will pray very much for them.

I recommend that you also be at peace and happy in the Lord and to pray for me and to recommend me to the prayers of the relatives and acquaintances, to whom together with you I send my last greeting.

I ask everyone one last time for pardon for the offenses that I have caused. I embrace you tightly in the Heart of Jesus together with all the family.

Forever your daughter,
Sister Maria Gabriella

Friday, 5:00 (April 21, 1939)

Dearest Mrs. S.,

I write you here near your daughter preceding the wedding journey. She is calm and often smiling, always sweet, almost immobile. I was also here during the night because she is at the end of her pilgrimage and this type of disease can prolong itself beyond every provision, but it also can be surprising. About 11:00 P.M., it seemed to me from her respiration that the Lord might take her. We called the Chaplain, a truly saintly priest, full of zeal and love in spite of his seventy years. When she saw him, Sister Maria Gabriella welcomed him with a smile full of holy joy. He brought her Communion at midnight, and then she rallied. We are here around her praying.

I just said to her, "I am writing your Mama." "Thank you" she answered me. She is united to the prayers with her mind and, even though suffering, when asked if she consents to suffer more if God desires it, she immediately says yes. When the Lord admits her to eternal union, I will telegraph you – and then rejoice and give thanks more than ever. You will have your daughter closer to yourself than when she was with you and more than now.

The Lord bless you. Thank you for your letter to Sister Gabriella and to me.

Sister Maria Pia

Wednesday, April 26, 1939

Dearest Mrs. S.,

With what desire you are waiting for this letter of mine.

With it you will also have the last writing of your daughter which she wrote at my advice and agreed that I would send it after her passage to the heavenly kingdom.

Mother Maria Gabriella had a visible decline from Thursday the 20th. Ever since Easter we have been keeping vigil at night with her, in spite of the pain she felt for being a disturbance. Thursday she was brought Holy Communion at midnight, as well as Friday, fearing the moment was near when it would be too late. Saturday morning was the improvement which preceded her passing. Then she began to suffer a great deal. Her body of twenty-five years and two months put up a strong resistance. She suffered with such meekness! Consenting to the acts of acceptance, of love, of offering that we suggested to her, Saturday evening she seemed at the end, but with full consciousness. She asked, with the trace of a voice that could barely be understood, "Communion, if possible, if possible." It was brought to her again as Viaticum. She was a little composed . . . But we remained all night, the Infirmarian, two other Sisters and myself — and the Chaplain also wanted to remain despite his advanced age. He did not want to leave her without accompanying her to the last breath.

After dinner on that Saturday, there was the providential visit of the Rev. Father Abbot, our Superior, accompanied by the Procurator General of the Order. The bishop also came and suggested giving a blessing to our young sick Sister. With much happiness he blessed her and commended himself to her prayers. She suffered a great deal throughout the night, but like a lamb.

About 2:00 A.M., she was calmed completely reciting the Office of Matins. She regained her calm breathing and delicate childlike expression. She remained like this for more than an hour, then the suffering resumed acutely. The Chaplain came after preaching to the community. He asked her if she wanted to receive Jesus. She became calm, smiled and during all of the preparation and thanksgiving I would repeat to her, "How good is the Lord! He loves you! Let us offer Him the dispositions of the Madonna's last Communion." It was her custom to say, "How good is the Lord" and she said it with an angelic expression that was touching.

Always worsening – but almost stationary, suffering very much and always sweet, modest, and dignified – she continued like this until afternoon. She looked at her already purple hands. She smiled as much as she was able. She kissed the Crucifix with long kisses when it was handed to her.

At 4:00 P.M. everyone went to Vespers, only the infirmarian remained. Then she entered her agony. The Sister, an excellent Religious (from Bitti) pleaded with the Lord, but with what faith! (she later told me) to prolong her [Sister Gabriella's life] until she had finished Vespers and returned. The Lord truly heard her! After Vespers I went to the infirmary with the entire community. The Chaplain came. We have the custom of sounding the agony by a certain ringing of the bell. They made a mistake and the two monastery bells were heard ringing for a feast. In fact it was the marriage feast.

At 5:30 P.M., very tranquilly she stopped breathing – her pulse lowered – as when, unable to speak she tried to say "yes." Then I lifted her up. She was already with the Lord whom she loved so much and to whom she offered the sacrifice of her young life for the union of the separated Churches.

It was Good Shepherd Sunday and the Gospel spoke of "the other sheep who are not in the fold and that need to be gathered in."

Cry, Mrs. S. You are her Mama. But thank, thank, thank the Lord. The burial ceremony took place yesterday. During the night we kept vigil in the Church with the two sisters from Dorgali and the others, two-by-two. Now she rests in the Monastery crypt which is found under the sanctuary. Her casket was put just under the altar.

Dearest Mrs. S., your desire for a photograph, so right and understandable, impressed me. The Chaplain tried one day, but it did not come out very well! However, in a manner befitting Providence, I was able to take it when she was laid out in the Choir. I could not do more – now she will be closer in spirit.

I will send you a rosary which I put between her hands while she was sick, and I told her that I would later send it to her Mama. "Thank you," she replied gratefully. It was blessed by the late Pope.

Jesus bless you, dear Mrs. S.,

Sister Maria Pia, OCR

Nashdom Abbey - April 29, 1939

Most Rev. Mother Abbess,

I had the intention of writing you immediately after I received your postcard, but it was impossible.

I am desolate to learn from our Rev. Abbot about Mother Maria Gabriella's death. I have continued to pray since I received the news that she had died. But I rejoice with her that the good God has accepted her sacrifice. I believe that this will be a sign of the greatness of the cause for which He, our Jesus, the Good Shepherd died. And He called her to Himself precisely on the feast of the Good Shepherd, didn't He? "And I have other sheep who are not of this flock. These too I need to gather and they will hear my voice and there will be one fold and one shepherd."

I cannot tell you how grateful I would be for some little memento of her that you could send me.

I would also like to point out that she went to the Lord on the feast of St. George, patron of England. It means that she will pray especially for our community and for our work for the return of England to true unity.

I told my friend Father Couturier of Mother Maria Gabriella's death. You can easily imagine how much we, and you feel united with the Holy Father Pius XII when he prays, *Da nobis pacem*! [Grant us peace] It is a real consolation to know that nothing in the world can disturb the hope of all Christians in His great prayer.

Your humble servant in Our Lord,
Benedict Ley

Grottaferrata, May 3, 1939

After the death of our little Mother Gabriella, I felt united to your community as never before. The night before her death, in which she suffered terribly, I put a small statue of the Holy Virgin on her bed. It is the same statue that I have on our work table. I put your holy card of the Sacred Heart at the feet of the statue. I made her kiss it while renewing the offering, and taking her hand, I traced her signature — think-

131

ing to send you this little memento after her death. You were so good to her — reciting for yourself and for her the Night Office from the time she fell ill.

Yes, Jesus called her to Himself this Sunday which has the Gospel of Unity. The fact struck me. She entered into agony at the hour of Vespers. Instead of ringing the bell at four intervals according to our custom, they made a mistake and rang the two bells at length. I realized it, but could not correct it because I was at some distance. Perhaps the Good God permitted it this way: for it was truly a wedding feast.

The little Mother left such a record of virtue that I have been asked to write some notes for the Novitiate. I do not know. I pay attention to the circumstances which the Good God inspires for me. Thank you for the prayers said for her. I add a photograph that was made at the request of her desolate Mama. My good Father, pray for us who are so united to your community after Mother Gabriella had made the bond of union.

Humbly,
Sister Maria Pia, OCR

Nashdom Abbey - May 9, 1939

I am an Angelican priest, monk of an English Benedictine community. Ever since I learned of your daughter's offering for the return of the separated brethren I have prayed for you. I hope that you allow me to tell you that your daughter's sacrifice impelled me to a greater fidelity to Christ and a more profound prayer for the reunion of all Christians under the Pope. . . . Perhaps it will console you to know that your daughter's offering has produced good among the Anglicans, many of whom ardently desire a corporate reunion with Rome.

I will pray much for you, Mrs. S. I confide you to the Mother of Sorrows. She who stood at the foot of the Cross of Jesus, will know how to sustain you and to console you in the loss which you have had. Let us remain united in prayer.

Humbly yours in Christ,
Benedict Ley

chapter 14
THOSE TWO JOINED HANDS . . .

I would have preferred to conclude these thoughts with the preceding chapter, with those bells of Grotta ringing for a feast.

For it is there that the unobserved, hidden, and brief adventure of Maria Gabriella concludes: at Vespers of Good Shepherd Sunday in 1939, in a poor and unadorned infirmary room, a little more than twenty-five years from her unobserved and hidden birth in the poor and unadorned dwelling of Dorgali.

These few pages which follow, compiled I confess a little unwillingly, are intended to be above all an act of consideration for the readers, who for the most part also want to know what happened at the end.

And they have the right to know.

Even more so because Gabriella is an attractive creature. First, she finds you distracted and indifferent, then she intrigues you, next she interests you. She then grasps you and when you have begun to understand her and like her, she suddenly goes away leaving you with a great sense of emptiness, depriving you of something that had become a part of you.

Here then are some brief notes and some dates to give a bird's-eye-view of what happened afterward.

The body was placed on a wooden bier according to the sober and austere custom of the Trappistines. She had a nuptial wreath of flowers on her head and was laid out in the Chapter Room where her Sisters took turns keeping a prayer vigil day and night.

In one of her last letters to her Mama, Sister Gabriella herself had described in great detail, with her luminous gaze of faith, all the spiritual riches that accompany "dying in this house of the Lord." And in one of the last "little flowers" (n. 197) we heard her say, "Now I can die peacefully," when she learned that permission was finally obtained to bury the Sisters within the walls of the monastery as is the Trappistine custom. Thus, she was among the first, actually the second, to be buried in the new crypt under the sanctuary, "and her casket," wrote Mother Pia, "was put just under the altar."

A "sign"? . . .

She remained there until January 15, 1957 when the entire monastic community transferred from Grottaferrata to a new location at Vitorchiano in the province of Viterbo. They did not want to abandon the bodies of their Sisters buried at the old building.

Since there was no other available place in the city cemetery of Grottaferrata, they asked and obtained the fraternal hospitality in the large tomb of the Franciscan Missionary Sisters of Mary.

Immediately after her death, Sister Maria Gabriella's tomb became the most sought out place by prayerful visitors.

The providential entrance into the Grottaferrata Novitiate in June 1939, just two months after Sister Gabriella's death, of one of the most brilliant Catholic writers of the time, the Sardinian, Peppina Dore (later Sister Maria Giovanna) gave Mother Pia the opportunity to have the first biography written. It was published in 1940 by Morcelliana with a Foreword by Igino Giordani. It was a sell-out and in a short time six editions were also sold out. A second biography, also by Dore, had a Foreword by Edward Fenu.

Also in 1940 a Bohemian author, Ivan Marianov, taking notes from Dore's book wrote a biography edited at Frjdek in Czechoslovakia, in the "Zivotem" series.

Biographies, many originals, were published rapidly in the United States, France, Belgium, Holland, Spain, Germany, Brazil, besides new Italian publications, among which the most complete, even if not always the most accurate, was that of the Jesuit Father Celestino Testore.

All of this effort to spread quickly the name and person of Sister Maria Gabriella in Italy, Europe, and overseas, in the Catholic world and in the heart of various Churches, was done precisely on the strength and in the name of her hidden offering for unity over which she had spread the veil of total silence.

Letters began to pour in, requests for holy cards, notifications of graces above all spiritual, spectacular returns to God and to the Church, sometimes narrated openly by the very people involved and attributed to the "little victim" of unity. Exceptional healings were unhesistatingly attributed to her intercession. They were sometimes ardently described as "miracles" in the simple and "profane" language of the beneficiaries.

All of this in the course of a few years, against all human foresight, has given rise to a general consensus about her character as to justify the so-called "odor of sanctity." Thus, when the Grottaferrata community transferred to Vitorchiano in 1957, it was simultaneously decided to ask the Holy See permission to introduce the Cause for her Beatification. The request was granted without any difficulty and in less than ten years, especially due to the ardent and untiring zeal of the Vice-Postulator, Father Pietro Cappio, it was brought to its conclusion. The ordinary as well as the apostolic processes, those notes from which we have extracted the "little flowers," were declared valid.

That allowed, among other things, for the opportunity to proceed to the canonical recognition of her mortal remains. This took place in Grotta on January 15, 1957, in the presence of two doctors, a bishop, two abbots, one abbess, the Postulator and Vice-Postulator. The long detailed verbal account records that the body was found "intact."

But what is surprising and regretful is that among such distinguished and qualified persons, not one had the bright idea to call a photographer or at least take a few snapshots in order to leave us, at least for the archives, a minimal photographic documentation. Nothing!

The coffin was opened, they looked inside, admired, prayed, blessed, then reclosed it and imposed the regulation seals. It was immediately buried with the others in the tomb of the Franciscan Missionaries of Mary. It was reclosed and sealed without any concern to do the minimum preservation work on those precious remains. This is still more surprising, and sorrowful than the missing photographs. How could nothing have been done when it is well known that at the opening of a coffin or sarcophagus the contact of the remains with the air triggers vitality in the bacteria? Where this is not immediately provided for by adequate means it leads inevitably to a fearful destruction.

This unfortunately happened to Sister Maria Gabriella.

The Lord permitted it this way. Perhaps it entered into his mysterious designs in the total oblation which Sister Maria Gabriella had silently vowed! The preservation of that frail, doubly consecrated body was a delicate sign of a tender predilection, even if in the absolute sense unclassifiable as a miracle. The second destruction of death overcame even the physical consummation of the holocaust.

Sister Maria Gabriella was able to re-enter the community in her own way on April 12, 1975. She found a new family than the one she had known.

Escorted and followed by a long cortege of cars, awaited by a multi-colored and cosmopolitan crowd of bishops, abbots, prelates, monks, religious women, brothers and sisters of all the Churches of the ecumenical world, by representatives of the laity and political sectors, and she who forty years before had timidly knocked at the enclosure of Grottaferrata, and left on tip-toe to the joyous encounter with her Bridegroom. That day she was welcomed in a festive way by the entire community and placed on a throne of flowers in the middle of the monastery Choir, while around the altar fifty priests concelebrated the Eucharist for the Unity of Christians.

After the ritual the procession crossed the cloister and her remains were carried to the new tomb. This time it was solely and completely for her within the enclosure, sheltered by the enclosure wall but visible also on the outside for the faithful and pilgrims.

A little more than a month later, May 28, the necessary permissions were obtained and a new exhumation took place. It was to substitute the wooden coffin which had remained exposed to the seepage of rain water in the grave at Grottaferrata, for it was not possible from an exterior examination to evaluate to what point the humidity might have penetrated to the interior.

If it is difficult to describe the tension with which we awaited with bated breath the climactic moment of the opening of the coffin, it is even more difficult to narrate the sense of disappointment and anguish that overcame us in the next instant.

The wood inside was intact.

But the remains of Sister Maria Gabriella were literally devastated by death.

It would be useless and in bad taste to describe it in detail.

Under the guidance of a venerated ninety-year-old specialist, Dr. Oswald Zacchi, who had more than two hundred similar experiences behind him, they worked for fourteen days with a preservative treatment on those poor remains. He cared for each smallest fragment with persistent patience and with infinite tenderness.

But there is one detail about which one cannot keep silent. The only part of the entire torso that was found intact, naturally in a state of calcification, were her forearms with the two hands joined in prayer still clasping the rosary beads.

After having "treated" those two hands with every means possible, a sculptor friend took a plaster mold, before they were returned again to their place. A new garment was brought with a new rosary, with the hope of at least saving those two joined hands from the last ravages of death.

Those two hands joined in the act of prayer help us to conclude worthily these pages faithful to the goal adopted at the beginning: to allow Gabriella to speak.

With those two joined hands and that worn-out rosary Gabriella speaks to us once again.

Yes, Gabriella of Unity, with those two hands joined beyond death in the act of lifting up to the Father the prayer of Jesus, "Father, may they be one!" "*Ut unum sint!*"

chapter 15

THE LITTLE FLOWERS OF MAÙ

V. Flowers of Heaven

The heavenly Father's loving designs upon Sister Maria Gabriella Sagheddu reveal themselves not only in the rapid ascent of her soul,* from her initial offering of monastic consecration until, under the inspiration of the Spirit, she made the generous holocaust of her youth, but also in the exceptional swiftness with which her brief life story passed from the total hiddenness of the cloister to the bursting notoriety of the ecclesial world, climaxing in her solemn Beatification on January 25, 1983, slightly more than forty-three years after her death.

The silent consummation of this little grain of wheat in the furrow of the Grottaferrata Trappistine monastery was accepted as a fragrant sacrifice of propitiation, and the richness of the blade, precociously matured in love, radiated within a short time unexpected light and grace, clear signs of the divine presence and action within her soul.

We report here some of the most relevant of these signs taken from the official documentation in the Archives of the Sacred Congregation for the Causes of Saints, beginning with the miracle which opened the way to her Beatification.

The Miracle

This concerns the miraculous healing of a nun of the Benedictine monastery of Alcamo near Trapani, Italy. The complete healing of Sister Maria Pia Manno, OSB of *double ocular retrobulbar neurite* is attributed to the intercession of Sister Maria Gabriella and took place at 5:25 A.M. on March 25, 1960.

---

* *The Holy Father proclaimed her heroic virtues on May 4, 1981, one week before the assault against him in St. Peter's square.*

The diligence and timeliness with which the Ordinary Process was opened at the Trapani chancery office, only one year after the actual event, permitted the collection of direct and immediate testimony, which was accompanied by original clinical documentation of special value.

The Ordinary Process took place at Trapani during 1961-1962 with the customary procedures prescribed by the Holy See. At the same time an Informative Process was carried out at the New York Archdiocesan Curia in 1962 in order to question one of the most important technical witnesses, Dr. Vita La Rocca, chief oculist at Columbus Hospital in New York, who had personally examined the healed nun just a few months before the miraculous event.

In January 1979, Sister Maria Pia Manno was summoned to Rome to be placed under an out-of-court clinical examination by the illustrious expert of the Sacred Congregation for the Causes of Saints, Dr. Camillo Pasquinangeli. His detailed and accurate appraisement, enriched by new and modern diagnostic assessments, were defined as "brilliant out-of-court reports." As an added advantage he had wisely reorganized the information.

Also in January 1979 a rescript from the Sacred Congregation for the Causes of Saints granted apostolic value to the Ordinary Process on condition that a new Informative Process be carried out at the Diocesan Curia of Trapani. In this process, which took place at Trapani in 1980, it was possible to question the cured Sister once again. More cross examinations of the Mother Abbess and other Sisters, previously examined at the Ordinary Process, were conducted by Dr. Francesco Caselli of the University of Palermo and were of primary importance. We therefore have a wealth of first-class testimony, accompanied by abundant clinical documentation. *(voto VII)*

Sister Maria Pia Manno was born at Alcamo on December 2, 1926 to Gaspare and Vincenza Grillo who had twelve children, six of whom died very young. She entered the monastery January 18, 1945, at the age of nineteen. In 1947 she began to have headaches, tiredness in reading, and trouble with her vision. She went to an eye-specialist who prescribed glasses for her, but the problem did not stop. She visited the doctor again and new glasses were prescribed.

Despite the glasses Sister's eyes became worse. When seeing her in May 1959, Dr. Caselli discovered "dystrophy of the retina and paleness of the optic papilla." She barely had 3/10 vision with the use of a corrective lens. In July 1959 she was examined by Dr. Vito La Rocca of New York who was living in Sicily at the time. Excluding every form of hysteria or any similar state, he diagnosed "a severe impairment" of vision in the patient: *optical retrobulbar neurite, in a "truly advanced" state* (*Summ.* #75-76), causing him to fear complete blindness in a short time. She went to Dr. Caselli again and he confirmed the previous diagnosis.

Dr. Bianco left no hope for improvement and predicted total blindness in the course of two years (*Summ.* #60).

For some time the Sister had no longer been able to read and participate in the recitation of the Divine Office in Choir.

The night of March 19, 1960, Sister Maria Pia had a dream. She saw the Servant of God, Sister Gabriella, who invited her to read the Office for March 25, the feast of the Annunciation. The pain in her eyes and temple increased during the following days until 5:00 A.M. the morning of March 25. She was discouraged, but she still had a thread of hope that the dream about March 25 might come true.

At 5:25 A.M., at the beginning of the reading of the Liturgy of the Hours for that day, she suddenly realized that she could read perfectly. With immense joy she took part in the entire recitation of the Office which lasted 1 3/4 hours (*Summ.* #14). Her Sisters were surprised and astonished.

From that moment on she no longer suffered any difficulty. She now reads easily even with poor lighting, and she performs all her duties of religious life as her Superior, Sisters and the many doctors who examined her until 1980 have certified. It was a complete, perfect, instantaneous, lasting healing that has been attributed to the intercession of the Venerable Servant of God Maria Gabriella Sagheddu. *(voto I)*

The peculiarity of this miracle consists in the fact that Sister Maria Pia did not have a special devotion to the Servant of God Maria Gabriella Sagheddu nor had she ever prayed to her to heal her of the almost total blindness. She was not completely ignorant of the Servant of God because she had been spoken of in the community and she had been prayed to for the reconciliation of two spouses who were separated. But Sister Maria Pia had not put her whole heart into that prayer, even though she did follow along with the grace of the moment. Whereas usually novenas and long prayers come first and the miraculous grace follows prolonged prayers, here everything happened completely opposite. Lacking any real confidence in the Servant of God's intercession, Sister Maria Pia offered no special prayers. The initiative, so to speak, was taken by the Servant of God herself who appeared to the blind sick Sister, who was taken completely by surprise, on the night between March 19 and 20, 1960. The Servant of God told the sick Sister that she would be able to read the lessons of the Divine Office on the feast of the Annunciation (March 25). The sick Sister did not have much faith in the dream. She passed from moments of euphoria and faith and hope to others of doubt: will it later be true or was it only a strange dream?

On the morning of March 25, 1960, about 5:20, she is in Choir with the other Sisters for the Office. She remembers the dream and suddenly she sees and reads without fatigue for about one hour and forty-five minutes. (The Office had not yet been reformed and shortened.) The Superior and all the Sisters were present at the phenomenon and immediately after Choir heard the account of the healing, including the preceding dream and its actualization at that moment.

To make the event even more surprising, Sister Maria Pia gave little importance to the healing as a miraculous event. She destroyed the paper on which she had written while blind the matter of the dream and the information about the future healing, without the least consideration of how it would serve as proof for the Cause. She said it was written "crooked" and so she tore it up.

Thus we have one certain, very certain fact: a Sister who suffered at least two years from progressive blindness and who had reached the final phase, fatally destined to total blindness, was suddenly healed in a total and definitive manner. The healing was foretold in a dream by Maria Gabriella Sagheddu. Everyone saw the blind Sister; everyone saw her suddenly healed, even if in that Choir on that morning there was no eye doctor with instruments to measure the healing process. But there is no need for objective medical reports to know when a blind person is healed, if she sees, if she reads, if she works, if she does things that she was absolutely unable to do before. Fortunately we have abundant documentation in the case released by the doctors who treated her and who noted, little by little, the gradual deterioration of the eyes by means of analyses, diagnoses, therapies, and so on. All of these numerous medical evaluations confirmed the obvious fact: a healing completely out of the ordinary and one that could not have happened naturally. *(voto IV)*

All the physicians interrogated in the process declared the immediate healing of *optical retrobulbar neurite* in both eyes as *not naturally explainable.*

After twenty years of investigations, assessments, and discussions that took place between the miraculous event (1960) and the conclusion of the Informative Process at Trapani (1980), the last obstacles were overcome in 1982 with marvelous rapidity. The affirmative vote of the Medical Consultation of the Sacred Congregation took place on January 21, 1980. On October 26th, the Congress of Consultors affirmed by unanimous vote the theological value of the miracle. Equally unanimous was the vote of the Cardinals on the following November 16th.

A month later, December 17, the Holy Father promulgated the decree *Super miro* and arranged for the Beatification to proceed. On January 25, 1983, Sister Maria Pia Manno, the recipient of the miracle, had the joy of assisting in person with her Abbess at the solemn ceremony of Beatification of her heavenly benefactress.

Graces of Unity and Peace

After the miracle we give first priority to the exquisitely spiritual "signs" which are linked to the particular *charism of unity* that characterized the specific mission of Sister Maria Gabriella in the ecclesial reality of our time.

Delicate details of the divine Bridegroom made her very death a contradiction: strange bells that rang out as for a feast instead of the customary death toll; and emanation of a delightful aroma which issued from the consumed remains of her unadorned tomb, and for days and nights and months imposed itself as an indisputable reality to the stubborn unbelief and prejudicial skepticism of some of the faithful. Even scholarly and austere prelates of the Curia, who were at first distrustful and indifferent, were eventually conquered and captivated by the proof of this unintentional evidence. Other signs were the irresistible charm which attracted other Christians of every confession; the profound call to the interior life and to prayer for seminarians,

Sisters, priests and bishops; the seal of reconciliation and restored harmony in the hearts of families divided and in conflict.

1) The Father Abbot of Nashdom, Dom Augustine Morris, wrote on June 4, 1959 to Pope John XXIII:

It is with special emotion that I, Abbot of an Anglican monastery, humbly dare to approach Your Holiness with the request that you declare to be among the Blessed the holy nun, Sister Maria Gabriella Sagheddu.

I have heard with the greatest gratitude of the heroic offering of her life for Christian Unity and I am a witness that her example has brought joy and inspiration to others, including Anglicans. Year after year the great understanding of brotherhood and the greatest love for their brothers and sisters of other Churches penetrates more and more among Christians. I believe it just, to attribute such a benefit, under the Providence of God, to those whom He inspires to offer their prayers and sacrifices to Him for this goal. Sister Maria Gabriella emerges from such a number in the fervor of her prayers and in the heroic nature of her sacrifice.

2) The already mentioned Father Master of Novices of Nashdom, Dom Benedict Ley, after being a pilgrim to Grottaferrata to pray with his Abbot at the tomb of the little sacrificial victim, then maintained with the monastery a close spiritual correspondence totally impregnated by a common ecumenical passion for the unity of Christians. On June 11, 1959 he wrote:

I acknowledge and truly believe that Sister Maria Gabriella offered her life for the supreme cause of Christian Unity, and that this offering was accepted by God. I know that her example has inspired, and will inspire, many Anglican religious and others to be fervent in prayer and sacrifice for the unity which Christ wants and by the means that He wants.

I attribute to the help of Sister Maria Gabriella Sagheddu's prayers the following intentions:

— my protection and preservation from serious injury in a derailed train wreck between Paris and Dijon, France in September 1947 while making a trip to Rome;

— a very cordial reception by the Abbess (Sister Maria Pia Gullini) and the Trappistines of Our Lady of St. Joseph, Grottaferrata (Rome);

—my friendship with Father Vincenzo Ceresi (Missionary of the Sacred Heart), official of the Secretariat of State;

—my interview with Bishop Montini (now Cardinal)* and all the good that I derived from that;

—my being received in a special audience by His Holiness Pius XII;

—the enlarging and increasing of my vision of Christian Unity as a consequence of my visit to the Abbey of Niederaltaich, Bavaria and my contacts there with the movement "Una Sancta" (in August-September 1955).

I attribute to the intercession of Sister Maria Gabriella Sagheddu the physical energy with which I was able to dedicate myself to the supreme cause of Christian Unity, despite a defective valve in my heart. I pray that she can obtain for me the grace to offer my agony and death for this cause, which is so dear to Your Paternal heart.

3) Bishops and priests also write that in those years, long ago, in the seminary they knew of the figure of Sister Maria Gabriella through Dore's biography. She was of decisive benefit to their priestly formation.

Messages of fraternal affection and ecumenical fervor come from the Protestant and Anglican Churches of the United States, Latin America, England, and Switzerland. These are joined with a continuous devotion to make pilgrimages to the tomb of the "little Sister."

4) Roger Schutz and Max Thurian, who in those very same years began the foundation of Taizé, come as pilgrims to Grottaferrata and pause a long time to pray at the tomb of the Servant of God. They are accompanied by Brother Roger's mother who will be joined to the Trappistine monastery of Grottaferrata by an intimate and lasting bond of friendship, sustained by a fraternal and intense correspondence and nourished by common prayer for unity.

5) The Rev. Richard Rutt of the English Church mission, while a theology student at Cambridge before his ordination to the diaconate in 1951, in his burning zeal for the cause of unity and

---

* *Later Pope Paul VI.*

144

attracted by the charm of Sister Maria Gabriella, went for three consecutive years to Grottaferrata in order to visit her tomb. He then remained closely united to the Trappistine community. He was ordained a priest in the Anglican Cathedral of Ely in September 1952, and thereupon was sent to the Anglican missions in Korea. In June 1955 he wrote the Abbess:

> Our Lord Bishop will receive my Benedictine oblation in July at Seoul in the name of the Father Abbot of Nashdom. In this way I will again find myself more closely bound to St. Benedict and the memory of Sister Gabriella.

He added that he was preparing an English version of the biography of the Servant of God. He was later promoted to the episcopal dignity, first in Korea and then in the Diocese of St. Germans at Trurs in Cornwall. In such capacity, he wrote Pope Paul VI a letter on July 11, 1978 in which he said among other things:

> The Servant of God Maria Gabriella Saghcddu gives an example of the most authentic ecumenical spirituality which has been of great value and service to our generation. She also constitutes a magnificent example of faithful intercession for the missions and especially for China.
>
> As an Anglican Bishop, a long time grateful for the inspiration received from her example and her prayers, and as Episcopal Visitor of the Abbey of Nashdom, I ask to be able to add my voice to those requesting permission for a dispensation of the fifty-year rule of Canon 2101 of the Code, so that the process of her cause at the Congregation for the Causes of Saints will not be postponed.
>
> I have the honor to remain a most devoted and most obedient servant of Your Holiness.
>
> Richard of St. Germans

6) An American Anglican seminarian, John Jay Hughes, was a student at the General Theological Seminary of New York City and a friend of Richard Rutt. He too, went to Grottaferrata during Holy Week 1951, attracted by the ecumenical climate that hovered about Sister Maria Gabriella. Here are a few passages from his letter directed to the Abbess of Grottaferrata on October 22, 1951:

I told you when I saw you last Spring that I expected to be ordained a deacon (Anglican) in September of this year. However, and certainly in great part following my visit to Rome, I have been led to consider more carefully and with greater liking, the nature and claims of your Church — which you call *the* Church, but for me is still the Roman Catholic Church. The problem that has tormented my mind (and that still occupies it considerably) is to know if, in the controversial questions between Rome and Anglicanism, Rome is right and Anglicanism is wrong.

Given that my mind is occupied with this problem and since I still did not feel able to commit myself completely and irrevocably to the Anglican position without further research regarding its basis in truth, I asked my bishop to postpone my ordination until I have returned here in the Spring. So I am still a layperson and continue my studies in this Anglican seminary in New York.

Now I am writing to you, Mother Pia, to ask if I can have your prayers and those of your community for the following intentions:

1) That under the impulse of the Holy Spirit I may be led to the fullness of the truth and I go wherever the truth leads me.

2) That I will not distance myself from what the Lord wants to reveal as his will for me, whatever it may be. That I remember always that *whatever* the Lord wants of me — whether to remain here in Anglicanism where he has placed me, or to submit myself to the authority of Rome — I will not be called to anything other than carrying the cross every day which is the vocation of us all *in hac lacrimarum valle."**

I also ask your prayers for my father, an Anglican priest, and for the other members of my family, who might take my eventual submission to the Church of Rome as a personal injury done to my family. My father always looks with extreme harshness at any Anglican who enters the Roman Church. There are also other Anglicans, searching and doubtful, who need your prayers. I will tell you the baptismal names of two that I know: D. and E.

---

* *Tr: "in this valley of tears."*

If you will unite your prayers to mine for the above-mentioned intentions, I will be immensely grateful to you. I also ask the intercession of the Blessed Virgin and that of St. Thérèse of Lisieux.

May the Lord be with you each day, dear Mother, and with the Sisters entrusted to your care in your hidden life of prayer and mortification.

On February 8, 1952, he wrote in a subsequent letter:

I have to tell you that a few weeks after I wrote you, one of the two friends I had mentioned (the one named D.), was received into the Catholic Church. He also realized that he did not have a vocation to the priesthood and in fact, became engaged and will soon marry a Catholic girl. Since he is no longer a seminarian he was called for military service. But he will probably not have to stay in the army more than a couple of years at the most. I hope that all of you will pray for him — above all that the Lord protect him in the midst of the temptations of military life.

I would like you to tell Mother Pia, when you write her, that I am very grateful for her letter and her prayers. My gratitude also goes to you and your Sisters in religion who have prayed for me. I hope that they will continue to do so, and I will continue to pray for all of you. On this earth we will never know how much our lives are influenced by the prayers of others: but perhaps we will know in heaven. It is also a source of great joy to think that we together (you at Grottaferrata and I, in America), even though separated by distance and, sad to say, by the ecclesiastical barriers, are nevertheless, in agreement, in some way, to fulfill the order of St. Paul: *Alter alterius onera portate, et sic adimplebitis legem Christi* (Gal 6:2).*

7) A well-known representative of the Waldensian Church, Franco Falchi of Torre Pellice, who already in 1933 had taken part in the meeting of the Oxford groups in London, knew of Sister Maria Gabriella by 1940. He was among the first to read

---

* *Tr: "Carry one another's burdens, and so fulfill the law of Christ."*

her biography. He was quick to write his impression to Professor Igino Giordani who had introduced her to him:

> I read and gave away copies of *Sister Maria Gabriella*. It is beautiful and moving: it fascinates me and I really feel at home. It acquires special significance in this hour of furious and raging passions. An exceptional creature in her humility, Sister Maria Gabriella places before us all the problem of the sanctification of the world, the re-christianization of the masses, the creation of modern saints through which God can reconstruct the Holy Church.
>
> On both sides there is the urgency of the saints who live in the world, of an integral, intelligent, inspired Christianity. Among the saints it is always understood and when this high potential of the Christian way will be reached, then the way of return will be divinely easy and joyous.
>
> It seems to me that Catholics have to "earn" this return, while other Christians must "want" it.
>
> In these words there is an entire program of prayer, reflection, inspiration, action which involves each one of us and can go very far.

After many years, in a letter of January 23, 1962, Falchi, recalling what he had written to Igino Giordani twenty-two years earlier, comments:

> "That program" that I sketched out at that time has taken me a long way . . . yes, a long way . . . to the goal, to the acceptance with infinite gratitude of the gift of total, complete faith that Mother Church gave me in 1953.
>
> I remember: the words you wrote me then were the echo of a conviction that I already had deeply in my heart . . . Then, it was all a succession of delightful discoveries, of clear dawns, of luminous certainties that have been as constellations on my spiritual journey . . .
>
> Sister Maria Gabriella!! It will be a great jubilee when she receives from the Church the prize for her heroic dedication to the cause of the Church!

The letter continues describing the most relevant phases of that long and slow journey "*that had led me to the goal*" and to the *special part that Sister Maria Gabriella has had in my life.*

8) The Brazilian schismatic Bishop Salomas Ferraz of Sao Paolo, Brazil, was born and educated in Protestantism and later became a pastor. He was a studious soul, inclined to the search for truth. He joined the *Igrejia Catolica livre no Brasil* (ICLB), separated from Rome and became bishop and Head. In his soul's long torment, he ended by asking to enter the Catholic Church together with many of his faithful. After having made a public and solemn profession of faith on December 8, 1959 before the Archbishop of Sao Paolo, he went to Rome in 1960 to renew in the hands of Pope John XXIII his full adherence to the Catholic truth and his obedience and his attachment to the Supreme Pontiff *(L'Osservatore Romano,* March 23, 1960).

Returning to Brazil, he wanted to give personal witness to the role that Sister Maria Gabriella had in his definitive direction by her character and by the prayers directed to her for such an intention by many religious souls. On the feast of the Epiphany 1961, he wrote the Holy Father asking him:

if it might be worthy to introduce the Cause for Beatification of the said Servant of God, Sister Maria Gabriella, and thus to have the consolation of seeing her raised to the altars like a precious jewel of the Ecumenical Council.

The very happy reverberations which the convocation of the Vatican Ecumenical Council has had everywhere and finally among dissenting Christians by a great reawakening of the Christian conscience, we certainly owe to the action of the Holy Spirit who is inspiring the Head and the members of the Church of which He is the life-giving soul.

It is, therefore, not foreign to this movement, this imploring action of so many souls who offer themselves in sacrifice to God in prayer, in silence and in the trials of the cloister.

Among these souls, without a doubt, emerges like a star of the first magnitude, Sister Maria Gabriella, Trappistine of the monastery of Grottaferrata, who offered her young life, with all its purity, enthusiasm and spiritual, above all supernatural, energy, for the great work of the union of all Christians. For that union, most Blessed Father, we have come and are working with all our powers. We desire to persevere in this work during the few years of life which still remain for us, animated by the example of Your Holiness.

The fame of sanctity that Sister Maria Gabriella has left

in her native land at the moment of leaving for her heavenly home, has reached us here in Brazil precisely when we were preparing our return to the Father's House. We remember that her example could not be useless and her valid intercession invoked by us.

Later he took part in the Second Vatican Council bringing the personal contribution of his long and weary journey.

9) The voice of the authoritative witness Bishop Igino Penitenti seems of the utmost interest. At the Ordinary Process he gave evidence regarding the phenomenon of the "perfumes" as well as the special graces he personally received:

About the year 1945, I went to the Grottaferrata monastery with two young men of whom one was a Protestant with a profound skepticism regarding the rumor of perfumes that issued from the tomb of the Servant of God. He asked personally to see the Abbess, Mother Tecla, in order to visit the tomb and to disillusion me. [Mother] told me it was impossible because the tomb was situated inside the enclosure and in order to visit it, the permission of the Holy See or Procurator General (who happened to be present in the monastery) was needed. I asked the Procurator, Father Barbaroux, for the permission. Even though we were united by a close friendship, he responded quickly and brusquely, in these terms:

"No way, you will want to believe in those fantasies too, and the hysteria of these nuts! And do not believe in those so-called perfumes!"

"But I only desire, if you permit, to visit the tomb and pray over it two 'Requiem'* with the two young men who have accompanied me."

"If that is so," he said, "I'll go too, since I've never been there."

That said, he called the portress, opened the trap-door in the sanctuary and by means of a little stairway entered the

---

* Tr: "Eternal rest grant to her, O Lord, and let perpetual light shine upon her."

crypt below where there were tombs of several deceased Sisters placed in very rudimentary ways. We were shown that of Sister Gabriella. We recited a "*De Profundis*"* and made the two young men go out first, then me, and last, Fr. Barbaroux. Just as I reached the steps to go up I began to look around because I was overpowered as by an invisible cloud of violet perfume. I also saw behind me that Fr. Barbaroux, as if a victim of a convulsion, almost did not want to believe it himself. He walked sniffing nervously with his nose. Then he saw my surprise and said, "You, what do you smell?"

"I smell an intense perfume of violets."

"No way do I want to believe these things. I bet either you or the two young men or some Sister has sprinkled some sweet-smelling essence or hidden some bunches of violets."

At that I added, "It could be that they sprinkle some sweet-smelling scents and we can investigate. In fact," I said turning my pockets inside out, "I don't have any little bottles of essence or perfume. Nor can there be natural violets because there aren't any here in August." The two young men declared the same from the top of the stairs, affirming they smelled the same perfume and they did not have any sweet-smelling scent or had they sprinkled any. Having gone up, Fr. Barbaroux hurried with me to inspect, smelling right and left if there were any vases of flowers around or anything that might give off a perfume. Not finding anything and closing the trap-door, he said, "Well, let's not say anything to the Sisters." And in fact, we didn't say anything to anyone at that time.

Permit me to note that in Russia where I was a military chaplain for the Italian Army, I had the feeling that the Lord wanted me especially consecrated to the ecumenical apostolate for the return of other Christians to Catholic unity. Going to her tomb, I asked Sister Gabriella to make me know by some sign if this was in God's plans, as a proof the feeling was truly the Lord's will in my regard. Therefore, I can say I was deeply convinced that those perfumes were a tangible sign for me of the divine approval of my consecration to the aforesaid apostolate.

---

* *Tr: Psalm 130, "Out of the depths I cry to you . . . "*

And he adds a little further on:

See how much happened to one of my penitents, Enrichetta Quarta, now deceased. She was advised that she would be dismissed from the Trappistine monastery of Grottaferrata because of illness. Once, sleeping in the infirmary in the same bed where the Servant of God died, she saw in a dream the Servant of God, who told her not to fear her departure from the monastery, because after a few months she would be re-admitted through the concern of a priest. In fact, she was given hospitality in my house for three weeks and through my interest was re-admitted and died soon afterwards. In my regard, I must mention that suffering from terrible constipation which caused me stomach troubles and almost uninterrupted throbbing headaches, I had recourse to Sister Gabriella to obtain relief. After a few days of prayer I was completely freed and until this very day I have always been well, except for a few rare headaches caused by other reasons.

Finally, I must point out that I have many times met religious souls tormented by passions contrary to chastity. I have suggested to them to have recourse to Sister Gabriella's intercession. I have always heard those same souls say that they found quick relief and spiritual comfort.

But the specific charism of Sister Maria Gabriella is "unity" evidenced not only on the ecumenical level, but also — repeatedly and with special emphasis — to resolve seemingly incurable situations of disunity either from God (states of serious temptations, or positions of obstinate refusal of the life of grace), or at the level of the local Church, or at the heart of the *ecclesia domestica*.* We refer here to the following few among the most significant cases. The original documentation is jealously guarded in the archives.

10) I am a girl who, after reading the magnificent and simple life of Sister Gabriella, was completely redeemed and converted: the first *true* miracle that occurred last year in autumn.

Afterwards I always prayed to my Saint and I obtained

---

* Tr: "domestic church."

other graces. Yesterday I finished a novena and again the miracle that I asked for happened. Everything I ask for — in the first place to be pure, good and constant — of Sister Gabriella, I obtain!

I receive Holy Communion almost every day and Sister Maria Gabriella takes me by the hand before the Lord. I am writing you this because I want you, good Mothers, to know the good that your Flower is doing.

Pray also for me. The world is so bad, especially for a girl who lives among so many people and always needs divine help.

S.P. (June 5, 1941)

11) I immediately felt attracted by the holiness of a person called to a life so similar to ours. But above all, I was conquered by her immolation for such a great ideal: the unity of the Church, especially because in my family there are members who belong to the Orthodox Church.

I immediately felt impelled to pray to her for the children of my sister who married an Orthodox man, and for my brother's wife, also Orthodox. While I prayed and fostered these desires, lo and behold, completely unexpectedly and *spontaneously*, my sister-in-law asked to enter the Catholic Church. This moved me, especially because she lives in another city and I had never been able to talk to her very long and confidentially about these things. In fact, I was not even sure of her feelings about religion in general, especially given that she is a medical doctor like her husband.

But I have to say, the dear little Saint surpassed my most ardent hopes. I did not even dare to speak of my great desire — it seemed to me such a distant and difficult event. Instead, even before the end of this summer it had already become a reality, certainly through the prayers of Sister Gabriella. In a way entirely unexpected, but so simple and natural, my sister-in-law expressed the desire to come here for a few days in order to be able to take the great step in peace and recollection. And here is a coincidence which is a confirmation that the work of Sister Gabriella is involved in all of this: Your letter, Most Rev. Mother, reached me the very same day in which my sister-in-law arrived.

Now all of us love and appreciate dear Sister Gabriella. I

venture to say that truly among us she finds a special understanding and admiration, because we live in a country in which the pain of religious separation is living and actual.

Sister M.S. - Spalato (November 24, 1941)

12) Fully consenting, Miss M. ran away from home with a young man. After about a month of marriage she declared that she did not want her husband any more. She nourished a ruthless hatred toward him. It was such an aversion that she would have killed him. This was not because he was a bad boy or that he had carried her off by force, since it was actually the girl who fled with him.

In these circumstances, in order to avoid the greater evil, they separated, after the parish priest and relatives had tried in every way to persuade the young bride by wiser advice.

The girl remained at her parents' home for a good eight months without ever leaving the house or wanting to see anyone. Think of the extreme suffering of all the relatives!

We began a novena with great confidence to Sister Maria Gabriella. And, *as soon as the novena ended,* the young bride completely changed and without human intervention asked to be reunited with her husband to the great joy and emotional tears of the entire family.

What people could not obtain, Sister Maria Gabriella obtained and we share it for the glorification of our protectress.

M.S. - April 23, 1959

(letter signed and authenticated by parish priest)

13) I am very happy to relate to you a spiritual grace that was so much awaited, and that we attribute to Sister Maria Gabriella.

With the dispensation of the Holy See, our community had accepted a girl as an inside oblate who was a little mentally deficient. In the beginning she behaved as a true religious, but after a few years, she became unbearable because of her behavior to the detriment of the common regular observance.

What was worse, she was attached to a Sister in a diabolical way. This could not be endured and so the said oblate screamed, cried, cursed, disrupting silence, observance and peace in the community.

154

The day on which a picture of Sister Maria Gabriella arrived was a very critical moment for me. I was not disposed to forgive and be around the oblate. Nevertheless she could not be sent away from the monastery because she was alone and an orphan. Before dying, her mother had given all her possessions to the monastery with the agreement of caring for her daughter. We suffered for several years because of this oblate's behavior and without a way out.

On January 25, 1960, *when the octave of prayer for Church Unity concluded,* I also received the life of Sister Maria Gabriella. She obtained for me the much desired grace for which I personally, and the entire community, gave thanks to the Lord. The Lord had heard us through the intercession of His Servant.

Everything changed. The oblate became a little lamb and completely transformed. Now we all feel reborn and regular observance is vigorous. After about three months, the said oblate continues more and more fervently and we hope that she will persevere with the help of Sister Maria Gabriella.

14) My two nephews became involved with relentless hatred in a law suit because of business interests. No human person was able to reconcile these hearts.

My religious words were not lacking and one of the nephews responded that if the Lord promised heaven if one made peace, or hell if it did not come about, he would have chosen hell in order not to have to pardon his enemy.

After two years, having invoked Sister Maria Gabriella that she might grant me this grace, I began a novena with faith, and on the *seventh day,* the favor was given. Now the relatives are happy and in holy peace.

I release the vow, with a prayer to publish it.

A.F. (January 21, 1961)

15) Out of a duty of gratitude and to the glory of God, I must express with full confidence everything that follows.

For about thirteen years I had to endure a serious unjust dispute in exchange for a true act of charity. It was carried out in the judicial tribunal.

I had fervent recourse to our Lord, the dear Blessed

Mother and various saints. But it was useless despite vows and exceptional promises. Heaven seemed closed to my supplications! Last February 20, I happened by chance to read in a newspaper: "Even time stops to pray at the tomb of the nun from Dorgali." I thought . . . I obtained the biography of the chosen soul and it moved me! So much so that I felt impelled to go immediately to Grottaferrata and venerate her sacred remains.

I was able to pray a long time at her tomb with keen satisfaction. I declared to my opponent the desire to settle the law suit solely for the triumph of the truth. A sleepless night followed. While I prayed to Sister Gabriella I had the inspiration that it would come true in the morning.

When reading the biography I marked the date of her death on my calendar with the intention of multiplying my prayers so that the conclusion of the case might be hastened. On *April 23* at 3:00 P.M., in the quiet of my room, I recited Vespers for the deceased nun and the Office of Readings. I went to Church to make a visit to the Blessed Sacrament. Leaving there, I met the lawyer who told me of my adversary's intention, until then obstinate, to cancel the case without any demands!

Today, April 24, the anniversary day of Sister Maria Gabriella's burial, I celebrated Holy Mass in thanksgiving for the chosen soul, after I had signed the settlement act and honorably concluded the case.

The event aroused astonishment because it seemed impossible to reach a solution, given the difficulties raised by the adversary and his proud and malicious character. Instead, everything ended unexpectedly . . . mysteriously.

I want to relate the grace obtained through the intercession of Sister Maria Gabriella, precisely on the day of her burial.

Bishop G. D. - April 24, 1961

16) I was alone in a room at work in order to free my office, when the door suddenly opened and an individual appeared who had tormented me for a long time. I was frightened at that moment, but the instant I invoked my beloved protectress, Sister Maria Gabriella, I no longer felt alone. I felt she was very near me. In fact, that person who was so badly disposed, said to me: "Are you praying to some saint?" I replied yes and gave the name.

"I came to carry out my plan, but now, no. Thanks to your saint."

On the following Sunday, he went to Confession and Communion, and asked my forgiveness many times. Now, at work I always have to be in the office with him. He shows me the greatest respect. Four months have now passed. He no longer expresses himself in either indecent words or acts.

I thank the dear Saint from my heart and I always try to keep the most lively remembrance: in moments of need she will be my powerful protectress.

Sr. L. M. - May 15, 1962

17) An event arising from the 1968-1970 youth rebellions: the harmony of the parish was suddenly disturbed. A painful wound to unity was born because of the argumentative attitude of the young assistant pastor. I thought: Sister Maria Gabriella from heaven can help rebuild unity in this local Church . . . In a short time everything returned to tranquillity and the same priest, with exemplary humility, recognized his mistake. Today he does good work as pastor in another area.

Other events regarding some families in serious crises wonderfully regained unity after praying with me to Sister Maria Gabriella, imploring her to intervene. Families are born from the sacrament and are the "domestic church."

For the record, I will say that it concerned the following five cases. (. . . omitted . . .)

The sign of Sister Maria Gabriella's heavenly intervention is in the swiftness of the change in souls whose brokenness is revealed as humanly incurable despite friendly help.

It seems to me that this is the peculiar characteristic of Sister Maria Gabriella's heavenly intervention: the area of unity of souls which is the most difficult.

Father R. D., pastor - January 18, 1982

18) One could continue at length recounting an uninterrupted chain of "signs" of a purely spiritual character. But in order to conclude this brief selection one cannot fail to mention the phenomenon — bordering on the miraculous — of the exceptional fruitfulness in vocations in the Blessed's community.

From Sister Maria Gabriella's death in 1939 when the world already rocked by the beginning of World War II, through the war and post-war desolation, to the conflicting times after the Council and 1968, the community of Grottaferrata (transferred to Vitorchiano in 1957) has never known a single moment of vocation crisis. On the contrary, it has had to divide three times in order to give life to three new foundations, all very flourishing: in 1968 at Valserena, Italy in the Diocese of Volterra; in 1973 at Hinojo, Argentina in the Diocese of Azul; and finally in 1981 at Quilvo, Chile in the Diocese of Talca.*

With all that, the community continues to be animated by about eighty members, almost double the number at the time of Sister Maria Gabriella. The novitiate is constantly populated with young professed Sisters, novices, and postulants. A little more than forty years after her death, Sister Maria Gabriella was the precise and sometimes decisive reference point in receiving the Lord's call for many of these young Sisters by their explicit declaration.

Marvelous Healings

The Postulation has received notification of hundreds of graces — above all, healings — formally attributed to the intercession of Sister Maria Gabriella. They are often supplied with clinical documentation and absolutely credible testimonies (of these, many carry verification and personal confirmation by the Ordinaries).

They concern the verification of events in the most varied parts of the world: from continent to island; from the Americas to the Far East. They date from the first months following the death of the Blessed, beginning in 1940 and continuing uninterrupted for the entire span of time until today.

19) In the sealed documents of the Apostolic Process on the heroic virtues of Sister Maria Gabriella, besides the Manno case, ample and detailed accounts have been reported. There is another acclaimed, sudden and definitive healing which no less borders on the miraculous. It concerns a Miss Mariangela Bosu in

---

* Tr.: In 1987 a foundation was begun in the predominantly Muslim country of Indonesia.

158

Marteddu, near Orotelli, in the Diocese of Nuoro, Sardinia (*Summ.* pp. 255-259). Already in November 1954, she underwent removal of the left kidney due to gangrene from multiple kidney stones. Six years later, in November 1960, she noticed the first symptoms of the same illness in the surviving right kidney. In the following months the problems became more serious until in September 1961 "there began very strong and frequent, painful spasms" which debilitated her in a short time to the point that she was confined to bed.

She was invited to Nuoro by the municipal doctor of Orotelli to be examined by a specialist, Dr. Giuseppe Dedola, a radiologist. He performed an ascending and descending pyelography which revealed a stone in the right kidney, with partial obstruction of the renal pelvis.

Her blood pressure rose to 190. The same specialist wanted to talk privately with her cousin, Antonio Marteddu — who later became her husband — to whom he declared that the illness was inoperable given the absence of the other kidney and he could not prescribe medicine in order not to weaken the suffering kidney.

Miss Bosu, who is still living today, thus describes the evolution of events on August 2, 1966 in her sworn report obtained for the acts of the Apostolic Process:

> I spent the entire month of October bed-ridden. Between the continual colics, anxieties and worries that bordered on desperation, I very much feared that I would soon die. I did not know how to resign myself completely.
>
> Toward the beginning of November, perhaps because of the retention of urine, my limbs began to swell, then my entire body including my face. A certain discoloring was also noted in the fingers of my hands. I felt a sense of suffocation and strong throbbing in my heart. I had the impression that my heart was spread out in various parts of my body. By now everyone agreed it was a desperate case. Father Antonio Bussu, then pastor of Orotelli, was actually notified of that. In the various visits he paid me, he exhorted me to confident prayer and also to resignation since the seriousness of my condition could not be hidden from me.
>
> On the evening of November 8, Father Bussu came to the house about 10:30 P.M. with his sisters and my friends Peppina

159

and Palmira. After exchanging a few words with those present, I asked if I could go to confession. The priest sent his sisters, my sister-in-law Brau Mariantonia and other people present from the neighborhood, among these Brau Giovannina in Rocca, her daughter Giovanna Rocca and step-daughter Mariantonia Rocca. After confession, he also gave me Holy Communion, promising to bring me the Holy Oils the next day. Then, giving me a holy card of Sister Maria Gabriella, Father Bussu repeated more insistently than other times during the last stage of my illness, the exhortation to invoke the Servant of God in order to be healed.

On the spur of the moment I resisted his suggestion, saying I was unworthy of such a favor, but he constrained me out of holy obedience, adding that it could also give glory to God. He allowed the people in the house to come back in again, then he urged them to leave me alone. He advised my sister-in-law to go to sleep. The priest also returned home with his two sisters.

After midnight, no longer feeling the harshness of the pain, my soul shook with contradictory feelings of fear and trust. I took the holy card from under the pillow and placed it on the painful place, the right side. I prayed to Sister Maria Gabriella that she would obtain for me from the Lord the grace to be healed. The painful spasm ceased at exactly that instant and I felt the need to get out of bed. There was an abundant elimination of urine, since I had not been able to expel any for several days.

At that moment, I felt relief and a great sense of gratitude to the Lord and Sister Maria Gabriella. I did not say anything to my family and friends. I lay down again, this time, on the side of my heart (I had not been able to do that since the time of my surgery), and I was immediately able to go to sleep. My sister-in-law called me by name about 3:00 A.M., but not having a response she feared that I might already be dead. She then approached the bed and listened to my breathing and shook me a few times to find out.

In the morning (November 9) I was able to go to the parish church and attend Holy Mass. The people were greatly astonished since, knowing the day before of my serious condition, they expected to hear the bell ringing for my funeral. I went to the cemetery in the afternoon accompanied by my sister-in-law, my friend Celestina Zene and others, in order to take part in the preaching mission which was being held there. I held out standing for the entire hour service, and afterwards made the way back, a distance of about one-and-a-quarter miles.

Father Bussu, for his part, wanted me to undergo a new radiological exam to verify the instantaneous recovery. On the 12th (I think) of the same month, I presented myself at the mutual Provincial of Farmers Rights for this purpose. From there, I was sent this time to the civil hospital of St. Francis in Nuoro to undergo tests.

After seven X-rays (five on that day and two the following day), I was given the medical report in a sealed envelope which I took personally to Dr. Dedola. He read it and told me, "There turns out to be nothing here of the stone. Only the cavity of the kidney appears evident where the calculus was before."

Following the medical report, the doctor wanted to prescribe a treatment for me. But, he explained, it was only preventative since I had a tendency toward kidney stones. I remember that I did not complete that treatment cycle. It caused me problems and I did not have any more treatments of that kind.

In the following years I had check-ups every four months: the kidney was always without stones. I regained my strength from that time. In 1963, I married and took up again the normal routine of my family duties, with some social work in the parish.

There are numerous sworn and reliable testimonies by relatives and friends and the pastor, on the sudden change from a state of kidney blockage with impressive symptoms of azotemic poisoning to an immediate, total and non-regressive activity and vitality. The event is generally attributed to the intercession of the Servant of God.

Successive radiological examinations carried out periodically each year showed in a clear manner that the single kidney, even though greatly overworked, never again produced new stones.

It is impossible to refer to all the other cases of *wonderful healings* and *extraordinary graces* attributed to the intercession of Sister Maria Gabriella. Some have also heralded from the most

161

diverse parts of the world, where the silent and hidden figure of the little Sister of Grottaferrata has reached as a clear witness of the admirable action accomplished in her by the divine Spirit. Even the swiftness and breadth of extension of these wonders is amazing.

We will limit ourselves to a brief mention of some "sample" cases which either because of the seriousness of the event or the fame of the person involved, can be considered among the more relevant.

There emerged the cases of favors obtained concerning the gift of motherhood: difficulty in becoming pregnant or carrying the baby to term; dangerous complications in gestation; difficult deliveries, frequently with unfortunate prognosis for the mother and the unborn infant. In many hopeless cases everything was resolved during a prayer novena. We will limit ourselves to two references:

20) Msgr. Benjamin Sole, pastor of San Bartolomeo in Ossi, Italy, Diocese of Sassari, testified on April 4, 1960:

Mrs. Maria Ventura in Fancellu, twenty-five years old, from Ossi was expecting a baby. She was seriously ill and urgently rushed to San Pietro hospital at Sassari. The doctors suspected leukemia. The terrible reply of the health officials was the impossibility of saving the mother and baby. The poor afflicted mother, full of faith, implored the Servant of God Sister Maria Gabriella, and the grace was granted. A baby girl was safely born. The mother was in excellent health and able to nurse the baby herself, something the doctors considered impossible.

21) With the confirmation and verification by his excellency Bishop Melas, then Bishop of Nuoro, Mrs. Rosaria Serra of Dorgali testified to the following:

In October 1943 I was in Sassari with my sister Grazia. She lived with her family for a considerable time, and I had gone for the coming joyful event and to provide assistance.

About two months before her due date, my sister began to feel bad. She grew worse and worse with the passage of the days, so that the longed-for event became a cause of worry for everyone.

These anxieties unfortunately showed themselves to be

more than justified. In her eighth month, and already in the clinic for a week, she suddenly became worse and it was clear that only a miracle could save her. She gave birth prematurely and was so weak, the medical personnel thought she was already dead.

That day the good Sister who cared for my sister did not hide from us the need to resign ourselves.

An operation in those circumstances was impossible and all hope to save her was lost. I left the clinic certain of impending catastrophe. Arriving home, I roamed through the rooms a little, unable to apply myself to any work. I searched feverishly for a relic of the Servant of God Father Manzella, intending to take it to my sister. While I was searching I found a holy card of Sister Maria Gabriella.

I returned to the clinic. My sister was still at the point of death with a fever of 106 and looking defeated. It was absolutely forbidden for us to offer her a sign or word. I put the holy card under her pillow and went home. The next morning I went to the clinic with a pounding heart. A great surprise awaited me. My sister spoke as soon as she saw me. She was out of danger!

"You know, Rosaria," she said to me with a weary smile, "last night I dreamt that we went together to the St. Paul book store to look for a book about Sister Maria Gabriella. Then I awoke. Everything was settled in my dream. I was freed from my poor friend death."

All of us, including the good Sister, remain convinced that that was a special favor from Sister Maria Gabriella. We have always silently thanked her.

As regards healings aside from illness sometimes considered serious or terminal, we cite the following cases in chronological order.

22) On April 23, 1940, the first anniversary of the death of the Servant of God, there was the unexpected and unhoped for healing of a very painful cold abscess on the leg of Miss Ilia Profili. The Mother Abbess of Grottaferrata, Mother Pia Gullini, at the Rogatorial Process of Freiburg, testified in these words:

Miss Ilia Profili, now deceased, in her youth was healed

of a cold abscess April 23, the first anniversary of the death of the Servant of God. I have related the event in a letter to the Vice-Postulator of the Cause (in 1958).

In the letter she mentions, Mother Pia explained in more detail what happened:

The young woman named Ilia Profili, daughter of Aurelio and Maria Pistoresi, was born on September 29, 1908 at Vellano (near Pistoia, Italy) in the Diocese of Pescia.

She was welcomed by Sister Benedetta, then in charge of the guest house, and given hospitality free of charge. It was February or March or April 1940. Did she already have the cold abscess on the leg? I do not remember. What I do remember well is that Sister Benedetta, who had already been infirmarian in the enclosure, took great care of that girl. She had her lie down on the sofa and kept a very hot bag on the leg. She went out for some fresh air with great difficulty and pain. It was well known around there.

She decided that she should go to the hospital for an examination and possibly a period of treatment. A private novena was begun to Sister Gabriella by Ilia, Sister Benedetta, two or three other Sisters and me. There was no improvement, so on April 22 after dinner she went to Rome. She had to sleep at a friend's house in order to present herself at the hospital at 8:00 the next morning.

She returned about 4 or 5:00 P.M. on April 23. As soon as she entered the door, jumping and shouting she called for Sister Benedetta. Sister Benedetta, an excellent religious, but of a matter-of-fact character and in the habit of going to the root of things, when telling me of the event laughed: "I pressed so hard on the tumor that was gone — that I caused another one."

Afterwards, Ilia told me what happened: "I suffered during the night — and slept little. I woke up at 5:00 A.M. — I prayed — and very slowly I moved my leg — thinking of the movements to make to get out of bed. But I did not feel any pain. Then I went to Church to thank the Lord and Sister Gabriella."

23) The witness Maria Mereu, a living childhood com-

panion of the Servant of God testified at the Ordinary Process of Nuoro *(Summ.*, p. 140, #143) that,

> . . . about 1941, my mother, Giovann'Angela Mereu, suffered vomiting and pains in her side. She even came to Nuoro, but no one knew a remedy to prescribe for her. She returned to Dorgali on the feast of Corpus Christi when she had the strongest attacks. I went to the parish church to have a Mass for the repose of Sister Maria Gabriella. I was promised that it would be celebrated the following day and at that moment my mother felt better.

24) Mrs. Grazia Fancello of Dorgali testified before the Bishop of Nuoro that in 1946 her brother Bartolomeo Fancello Secu,

> . . . fifteen years old, had an echinococcus cyst on his lung. One evening he was hemorrhaging profusely, but the doctor succeeded in stopping it. The doctor was very cautious, fearing another incident. At 9:00 A.M. the following morning a new blockage brought him to the brink of death. It seemed there was no more hope of saving him. A relative then told the parents and other family members: "If you have confidence in the help Sister Maria Gabriella can give us, I will go and ask her Mama for her rosary beads."
> Everyone, full of confident hope, accepted the proposal. While this relative was returning with Sister Maria Gabriella's rosary she met the pastor Father Meloni who was going to the sick boy. A little afterwards the pastor himself came to announce that the boy recovered after Father Meloni had put the rosary under his pillow. The sick boy sat up in the bed and asked for a little milk. He got out of bed the next day to the amazement of everyone.

25) The Rev. Father Antonio Bussu, first witness *ex officio* in the Rogatorial Process of Nuoro, gave the following evidence under oath *(Summ.* p. 153, #459).

> I remember that when I transcribed the letters of the Servant of God, my mother had the opportunity to come to know her. She suffered for seven years from a festering wound in the right sub-occipital region of her skull which caused her unbearable pain. She tried to cure it with oint-

ments, but she had no improvement. Earlier I had been a little skeptical of the extraordinary life of Sister Maria Gabriella, but one day in order to test her virtue, I took a holy card and prayed to her during the night, asking her for the grace of a healing. The same night the pains ceased. The wound healed in a short time and she had no pain for about a year. Then she became scrupulous for having renounced the merits of suffering and asked to suffer something again, although less than before. The same day she felt the pain again, which although not as strong as before, recurred periodically. The wound, however, did not reappear.

26) From Ascoli Satriano (near Foggia, Italy), Miss Pierina Pignataro testified in this way:

On Thursday, September 19, 1958, my uncle, the lawyer Armando Pelini, had a serious heart attack. The doctors considered the case difficult and ordered absolute immobility for four months.

I then turned confidently to Sister Maria Gabriella, whose name I had become acquainted with during my residence in Frattocchie.

The serious crisis was overcome. However, every Thursday there was a new complication added to the heart disease. The cardiograms always turned out more worrisome, until the doctors decided to put the sick man in a clinic at Foggia in order to treat the sudden irregular heart beats. Unfortunately, things did not improve even in the clinic. The night of December 8, 1958, my uncle mentioned a strong pain in his heart. I made an emergency call to a specialist. They gave the sick man several injections, but I saw that the pain did not stop. He said that by now there was no more hope and the family should be notified.

But I did not lose heart and began to pray with great faith to Sister Maria Gabriella, trusting in her help. My ardent prayers were heard. Toward morning, the sick man improved unexpectedly and thus he set out on the way to recovery.

Such testimony was supported by the following declaration of the attending physician, Dr. Efrem Jascone:

January 29, 1960

I declare that the lawyer Armando Pelini suffered a serious form of heart disease complicated by irregular heart beats (flutter, which in a few moments put his life in serious and desperate danger).

Even eminent cardiologists of the Roman school (Cassano, Puddu, Mussapia) who attended him, had judged as exceptional his remaining alive and the fairly good recovery of his cardio-circulatory system.

27) Among the various cases of cancer healings, we report the following declaration by Miss A. P.:

Since 1959 I was seriously worried about the health of my very beloved brother A. We feared a serious illness. But with deep trust I turned to the Lord through the intercession of a venerable nun whom I love very much, Sister Maria Gabriella.

On August 21, 1959, I decided to take him to the hospital in Brescia, where a *biopsy* was performed. The results were positive for *cancer* of the tongue. He then underwent radiation treatments.

I did not hide my alarm even if it was accompanied by a great faith in God. While my dear brother went to the same civil hospital in Brescia at periodic times, precisely June 20 — June 24, 1960 and November 27 — December 5, 1961, I intensified my prayer and asked the spiritual help of many religious souls and friends. I asked them to beg for the grace of healing through the intercession of the Venerable Sister Maria Gabriella, from whom I was certain of obtaining special help.

Knowing that acquaintances struck by such a disease had gone to heaven, I very much feared the same for my brother . . . but I prayed and had others pray. Now, after six years, A. is very well. The tests show everything is negative and my heart exults for joy when I think about it!

28) Father Charles Boyer, so well known in the world of ecumenism, and who wrote the preface to the second biography of Sister Maria Gabriella, was personally the object of two important favors as brought out in the Tuscolano Ordinary Process *(Summ.* p. 77, #222):

167

I remember favors received by Father Charles Boyer who appealed only to the intercession of the Servant of God: a healing from pneumonia contracted at eighty years of age and a healing of a broken leg at the same age.

29) Miss T. S. of Pianiga, near Venice, Italy, writes on April 16, 1981, asking spiritual graces for her family:

I have been sick for more than thirty years. On February 18 of this year I had my tenth operation. I know that I will have another two years before I am out of danger from the surgery I had three years ago and for which I had eight series of chemotherapy. But it is not of this that I want to speak, because I promised Christ to accept everything He wants to send me, provided that I survive my Mama, who is also very sick.

I am writing you because of this: a friend of mine gave me a holy card of Sister Maria Gabriella and the day I had the surgery I saw her in front of me. She placed her cool hand upon my hot forehead, and I opened my eyes and saw her. Then she asked me how I was, and putting her hand on my forehead again, she said these words to me: "Be strong and courageous. I will pray for you." I know that I have to be strong, even if at times it is hard, but I promised and I must keep going until the end whatever it costs. And I really hope that Sister Maria Gabriella helps me to keep going until the end.

And here we have finally, some important graces to road accidents.

30) I, the undersigned, Antonio Onnis di Ignazio, an elementary teacher at Quartu Sant'Elena, Sardinia, relate the following from a debt of gratitude to Sister Maria Gabriella.

November 4, 1952 about 2:00 P.M., while taking my brother from Quartu Sant'Elena to Flumini on a motorcycle, we hit a wagon. I hit my right leg against the wheel axle. When I realized (a few seconds before) what was going to happen to me, I cried out in a loud voice to Sister Maria Gabriella. The impact broke my right leg below the knee and the heel went in between the spokes of the moving wheel. It stripped the flesh to the bone and broke the fibula of the same leg.

A passenger car took me to the city hospital of Cagliari, while my brother went home to announce the accident. They treated me at the emergency room and took seventeen stitches in the wound. The X-ray showed a fracture of the tibia and fibula, and farther down (about six inches) another fracture of the fibula.

On November 6 they gave me a general anaesthesia and put it in a cast. The doctor spent almost three hours resetting the leg. At a certain point my heart failed and oxygen was needed. My mother continually invoked Sister Maria Gabriella.

I recovered gradually, remaining as a patient in the hospital for sixteen days. At this time a priest gave me a picture of the Servant of God that he had received from the Trappistine nuns. I slipped it down between the leg and the cast I had to wear for two months, until it was impossible to find the holy card. The doctor kept postponing taking off the cast, and so four months passed by. On February 20, 1953 the doctor sent me word to come to the hospital. While I was preparing to go, I slipped my hand in the cast and with great surprise found the holy card. I went to the hospital and the cast was taken off. I immediately walked around and was able to resume teaching without feeling the least pain or other problem. It is noteworthy that I had no massages or other therapy required in similar cases in order to reactivate the working of the injured joint. I could walk very well.

Despite having had the leg in a cast from November 6, 1952 until February 28, 1953, I did not suffer even during the winter. The healing was complete through the powerful intercession of Sister Maria Gabriella.

31) In March 1956, Caterina Pira returned from the fields carrying on her head a large container of wet clothes. It slid from her head falling on her left forearm breaking the radius bone. The pain was unbearable, making it impossible to work or rest. Nevertheless, she did not go to consult a doctor, thinking to treat it like a bruise. An X-ray, taken a few months later, revealed a fracture already mended, but incorrectly. The pain and inability to work persisted and it went on like this for a year despite the remedies performed.

On May 5, 1957, the commemoration of Sister Gabriella was held at Dorgali. The patient's mother, Mrs. Carmela Mereu, wanted to go to church with the specific intention of attending holy Mass and asking Sister Maria Gabriella for her daughter's healing. The next day, the daughter already felt better; another few days and the pain completely vanished. Now she can work as before without feeling the least problem. Her mother attributes her daughter's healing exclusively to the intercession of Sister Maria Gabriella.

32) The pastor of Lanusei, Father Mario Mereu, has left the following statement:

June 24, 1966, 4:00 P.M.. At the Lanusei-Nuoro State School a boy fell unconscious on the asphalt: Sebastiano Sette was unexpectedly struck by an automobile while crossing the street. A Roman traveling salesman immediately attended his wounds, transporting him to the nearby city hospital of Lanusei. The accountant Mr. Pietro Setzu of Lanusei accompanied the boy supported by his father Mr. Severino Sette.

After accurate examination and X-rays, the health officials found severe damage to the boy's spleen. He underwent surgery and they removed the spleen. Everyone hoped for the best outcome of the operation; but suddenly on Thursday, June 16, a complication worried the health officials. The entire morning they desperately took turns at the boy's bedside, in the attempt to save him from almost certain death. About noon, the health officials lost all hope of saving him and turned to his parents: "We have done all that was in our power," they said, "only a miracle can save him." In fact, there was no reflex or reaction from the sick youth, only the very heavy breathing which foreshadows death.

It was at this moment that I thought of seeking the intervention of the Servant of God Sister Maria Gabriella. I spoke to the frightened and desperate parents and put a holy card with a relic of the Servant of God next to the dying boy. I distributed leaflets to those present, to the sick and to the Sisters, asking all of them to ask the Sacred Heart of Jesus (it was the vigil of the feast) for this grace through the intercession of Sister Maria Gabriella.

170

I telephoned all the religious houses in the city, begging the Sisters and personnel to unite themselves with our prayers to save the boy, always through the intercession of Sister Maria Gabriella. Then I went to the hospital chapel with the boy's parents, where we prayed with great faith and the sincere assurance of being heard.

Returning to the bedside of the dying boy, the parents still in tears were already thinking of taking their son home so he could die within those familiar walls. I decidedly opposed this, saying that there was still a thread of hope until he breathed his last.

The hospital staff took turns monitoring the development of the fatal crisis, but despair could be read in the faces of everyone because of the impossibility of snatching dear Sebastiano from death.

Returning to the seminary, I found the seminarians in the courtyard and I invited them into the chapel where another confrère of mine, Father Pietro Vinante, had them pray in this way: "Sister Maria Gabriella obtain for us from the Sacred Heart of Jesus the health of this boy, for your glorification and for the cause of Church Unity." Father Pietro Vinante even asked the children from the nearby elementary school to snatch dear Sebastiano Sette from death.

I then took the Ritual and set out for the hospital again, intending to say the prayers for the recommendation of his soul (he had received the Sacrament of the Sick the evening of the accident). When I arrived there, I noted the continued gravity of the situation. We invited everyone to pray with faith. The holy rosary was recited. We all felt like a family and a great faith permeated the hospital wards. At the second mystery, the boy suddenly began to move and open his eyes and speak to the amazement and consolation of everyone, especially his weeping parents. The health care personnel, returning from the evening rounds, found the crisis overcome. The fever of 106 which had devoured the boy decreased to 100 unexpectedly. Joy overflowed our hearts and from that day Sebastiano Sette (known as Ninetto), continued to improve and returned home from the hospital after eighteen days. Now he enjoys excellent health, though still recovering.

The director of the hospital, Dr. Giacomo Spano, whom

I questioned about the case, responded: "The overcoming of the crisis which saved Sebastiano Sette enters within the powers and possibilities of nature (and therefore was not a miracle). However, I am firmly convinced without a doubt that a supernatural power assisted and enlightened us correctly in the timely preparations and remedies without our foreseeing the certain effects. God, acting upon secondary causes, snatched the boy from death."

We concluded this necessarily incomplete exposition with the authoritative evidence of Bishop Felice Beccaro, at that time Bishop of Nuoro, who testified at the Tuscolano Apostolic Process about the favors he himself received *(Summ.* pp. 3 & 4, #8-9). He testifies:

33) I am in a position to testify, and I gladly testify, that already in 1940, and even more in the following years until I left Sardinia, the fame of the holiness of the humble, great and generous Trappistine of Grottaferrata, heroically immolated for the unity of the Church, has spread and circulated with increasing amazement in the Nuoro area and the entire island.

To increase and spread such fame of holiness, detailed accounts of favors obtained through her intercession were validly assembled. And I am happy to refer conscientiously to a few personal cases for the glory of God and his faithful Servant. I do not remember the exact date because at least sixteen years have passed.

One Sunday I had to make a visitation of the parish of Ottana in the Malarica region, about twenty-five miles from Nuoro. On the preceding Sunday I had a strong attack of fever which alarmed my friends who agreed in suggesting that I cancel everything. I did not know what to decide. The fever continued late into the evening, so I recommended myself to Sister Maria Gabriella with confidence, almost impertinence. (I was her bishop!) . . . I went to sleep with a sense of peace . . . The next morning, I recovered from the fever and was in condition to leave, celebrate, confirm, preach, make the regular visitation and return peacefully to the bishop's house. I consider the event as a grace from Sister Maria Gabriella.

A few months afterwards, I returned from Orani to Nuoro

in a bus and sat near the driver. The bus came to a standstill in the Diocese of Oniferi because of a broken piston. After many useless attempts, the driver informed the travelers of the impossibility of continuing and telegraphed Nuoro. After at least an hour's wait, I had the inspiration to pray to Sister Maria Gabriella to free us from the trouble. After a few prayers I invited the driver to get back on the road. The bus responded immediately. It left, ran normally more than thirteen miles and entered a garage where another bus came to our rescue, responding to a telegraph from Oniferi. The driver spoke of a miracle. It was certainly a beautiful grace that I will never forget. I also add, as a debt of gratitude, that in the years spent at Nuoro, in the face of unfailing difficulties of pastoral administration, I quite frequently appealed privately to the intercession of Sister Maria Gabriella. I am convinced that that angelic Trappistine from my diocese helped her bishop from heaven.

chapter 16
FOUR PRIMATES

JANUARY 25

(*From* L'Osservatore Romano *January 26, 1983 and other publications.*)

The Octave of Prayer for Christian Unity concluded on Tuesday, January 25, with a solemn papal ceremony in the patriarchical Basilica of St. Paul Outside the Walls, presided over by the Holy Father. In order to make this special moment of prayer, offered by the Church for the full union of all believers in Christ, even more significant, the Holy Father chose the Basilica of the Apostle to the Gentiles. He also associated this liturgical commemoration of Paul's conversion, which concludes the Octave of Prayer, with the Beatification of Maria Gabriella Sagheddu, a young Sardinian Sister who gave her only possession for the cause of ecumenism: her young and brief life. Indeed, Sister Maria Gabriella is remembered today as "Maria Gabriella of Unity."

In the Basilica on the Via Ostiense, unusually crowded with about ten thousand faithful and pilgrims of every class coming from every part of the world, were Christian brothers and sisters of various confessions of faith united in an authentic and profound bond of charity.

In the reserved first row to the left of the papal altar, the section for honored guests, were qualified representatives of the Anglican, Lutheran, Episcopalian and Orthodox churches. Some were accompanied by a representative group of their respective ecclesial communities. Among many others, it was easy to recognize the prior of Taizé, Brother Roger Schutz with a group of his young monks; Canon Howard Root, representative of the Archbishop of Canterbury to the Holy See; Canon David Palmer, Rector of the Anglican Church of All Saints on the Via del Babuino; Rev. Douglas Ousley, Rector of the American Episcopal Church on Via Nazionale; Rev. Christopher Meyer, Deacon of the Italian Lutheran Church and Pastor of the Lutheran community of Rome; the Abbot of the Anglican Benedictine Abbey of Nashdom, Dom Wilfred Weston; and Bishop Dimitrios Psialmparlis, representative of the Orthodox Church at Madrid.

Among the civil authorities, besides the official delegation of the Italian Government, from the Prime Minister to the Vice-President of the House of Deputies, the Honorable Scalfaro, there were almost all the members of the Diplomatic Corps accredited to the Holy See. Italian Catholic Action was represented by the National President, Professor Monticone and the Vice-President Annalisa Aicardi.

More than 1,500 pilgrims arrived by every means, from the new Blessed's native land, guided by all the archbishops and bishops of Sardinia. Also from Sardinia were present the highest civil authorities: the President of the Region with all the aldermen; the Prefect of Nuoro and the President of the province with group leaders of all the parties; the mayor and aldermen of the town of Dorgali with the city's banner. The presence of the closest relatives of the new Blessed was of exceptional interest: her brother Salvatore; her sister Giovanna with her husband Giovanmaria Mesina, together with their daughters and a circle of grandchildren, three of whom received their First Communion on this occasion from the hands of the Holy Father. Her brother, Salvatore, and brother-in-law, Giovanmaria, also received Communion from the hands of the Holy Father. It was to them that in almost every letter Sister Gabriella had recommended, apparently in vain, sacramental encounter with Christ. The Lord has his time and the little Sister of Grottaferrata would never have been able to imagine with what royal generosity her prayer, which she was not permitted to see granted, would be crowned on this day.

The Holy Father arrived at the Basilica a little after 5:00 P.M. To welcome him at the right of the quadriportico were the Cardinal Vicar Ugo Poletti; the Pontifical Delegate for the Basilica, Bishop Antonio Mauro; the Abbot General of the Cistercians, Father Kleiner; the Abbot of St. Paul, Dom Giuseppe

Nardin. From the immense nave the voice of the people arose in the traditional Sardinian song, *Deus ti salvet Maria,* while the Holy Father walked in procession to the altar preceded by the concelebrants: Cardinals Carlo Confalonieri, Ugo Poletti, Ferdinando Antonelli and Bernard Gantin; Bishops Luigi Boccadoro of Viterbo, Giovanni Melis Fois of Nuoro and Luigi Liverzani of Frascati; and the Abbot General of the Trappists, Dom Ambrose Southey. The Holy Father presided over the introductory rites when he reached the "cathedra." Bishop Luigi Liverzani, the Postulator of the Cause of Beatification Father Paolino Beltrame Quattrocchi and the Consistory Advocate Giulio Dante approached the cathedra to ask the Holy Father to proceed with the Beatification of the Venerable Servant of God Sister Maria Gabriella Sagheddu about whom Bishop Liverzani read a short biographical account. The pope followed by pronouncing solemnly in Latin the formula of beatification:

At the wish of our brother Aloysius Liverzani, Bishop of Tusculano, and also of many other Brothers in the Episcopate, and satisfying many of the faithful, having consulted the Sacred Congregation for the Causes of Saints, by Our Apostolic Authority we grant that the Venerable Servant of God Maria Gabriella Sagheddu may be called Blessed in the future, and that the feast day of her birth, April 23rd, may be celebrated each year in the places and manner determined by the law.

When the two paintings of the new Blessed were uncovered for the veneration of the faithful the applause of the crowd was an overwhelming explosion. The painting inside the Basilica over the pontifical throne harmonized perfectly with the color scheme of the mosaics in the apse. This work of the Romanian painter Camillian Demetrescu, portrayed Sister Gabriella of Unity as an intercessor, under the light of the Holy Spirit, between the Anglican Cathedral of Lincoln and the Orthodox Cathedral of Santa Sophia. The painting on the exterior facade by the Dorgalese painter Pietro Mele, shows her standing in a flock of sheep pointing towards the classical figure of the Good Shepherd.

After the singing of the "Gloria" and the proclamation of the Word of God, the Holy Father gave the homily which we reprint below in its entirety, climaxed by the choral singing of the "Credo."

The six invocations of the universal Prayers of the Faithful, announced in Polish, English, French, Russian, Italian and Chinese concluded the Liturgy of the Word.

The celebration, at which twenty-four cardinals and numerous archbishops and bishops from every part of the world assisted, then proceeded with the Liturgy of the Eucharist. The Holy Father personally distributed Communion to the servers, as well as to the family members of the new Blessed, representatives of various pilgrimages, some Trappistine nuns who had lived with the Blessed, the "miracle" Sister and a few others, while an army of priests provided Communion for the large assembly of the faithful.

Before leaving the Basilica the Holy Father greeted the persons who had taken part in the ceremonies and the representatives of the Christian Churches.

Then in the Basilica Art Gallery (Pinacoteca Hall), the pope visited briefly with the civil authorities, with representatives of the relatives and acquaintances of the new Blessed, with representatives of the Trappists, Cistercians, Trappistines, and the Young Women of Catholic Action. The pope was also shown the numerous gifts offered by the postulation, the fellow-citizens and Sisters of Sister Maria Gabriella. He stopped with special interest and approval in front of the large bronze reliquary made by the sculptor Adriano Ambrosioni. It is mounted on an olive panel and represents in high relief "those two hands joined" of Sister Maria Gabriella intertwined with a rosary. Its silver cross contains a precious relic of the Blessed.

The Words of John Paul II

Here is the text of the homily delivered by the Holy Father:

1. The liturgical celebration of the conversion of Saul of Tarsus makes us relive the dramatic moment of his personal encounter with Christ the Lord, when the bold disciple of Gamaliel, "a staunch defender of God" (Acts 22:3), struck on the way to Damascus by the unmistakable voice of that Jesus whom he was persecuting without being aware of it, was immediately open to listen to his word, and at that very moment in which he submissively accepted the Divine Master's sad reproof, he was made his "chosen instrument to bring my name to the Gentiles and their kings and to the people of Israel" (cf.

Acts 9:15), in the capacity as his "witness before all men" (Acts 22:15).

The central element of the whole experience is the fact of conversion. Destined to evangelize the Gentiles "to turn them from darkness to light and from the dominion of Satan to God that they may obtain the forgiveness of their sins" (Acts 26:18), Saul is called by Christ, above all, to work a radical conversion upon himself.

In fact, Christ—who appears to him as a "light more brilliant than *the sun*" (Acts 26:13)—summons him in his heart, calling him by name, with a strictly personal conversation that leaves no room for ambiguities or escape: "Saul, Saul, why do you persecute me? It is hard for you to kick against the goad . . . Get up now and stand on your feet" (Acts 26:14, 16).

And Saul, who let himself be unsaddled by Christ and remained blinded by the unexpected experience of him, thus begins his laborious road of conversion that will last as long as he lives, beginning with unusual humility with that "What must I do, Lord?" and docilely letting himself be led by the hand to Ananias, through whose prophetic ministry it will be given to him to know God's plan.

2. This plan is summarized in the Lord's words: "I myself shall indicate to him how much he will have to suffer for my name" (Acts 9:16). With this brief gesture, like lightning in the night, Christ for a moment lifts the veil on the Apostle's future, allowing him to catch a glimpse of the privileged call to share in a singularly intense way in the mystery of the passion and cross. This sharing will be so full and vital, within that Mystical Body in which he has become a member through divine mercy, that Paul will be able to write to the Colossians: "Even now I find my joy in the suffering I endure for you. In my own flesh I fill up what is lacking in the sufferings of Christ for the sake of his body, the Church" (Col 1:24).

From that moment the former persecutor will become the evangelizer *par excellence* of the crucified Christ, of the "folly" of the cross, of the mystery of sin and of redemption in the Blood of Christ, of his death and resurrection, to the point of being able to say, "I have been crucified with Christ, and the life I live now is not my own; Christ is living in me" (Gal 2:20).

There is still an element in the episode of Saul's conversion that I feel urged to underline: it is the mention of prayer, the basis and foundation of every preparation and every apostolic activity. To allow Ananias to identify Saul, the convert, the Lord offers him an unmistakable sign of recognition: Ananias will find him in prayer. "At the house of Judas ask for a certain Saul of Tarsus. He is there praying" (Acts 9:11).

3. It is great reason for joy to observe that precisely these three facts emerge from the narration in the Acts: conversion, the cross, and prayer are essentially the elements on which the movement to restore Christian unity is based. Here at the tomb of the Apostle of the Gentiles, concluding the week of prayer with this ceremony that sees us assembled in a deep bond of charity in the one and same Christ the Saviour, we must together rebuild ourselves with these elements. In saying this, I am sure I am voicing the sentiments of the brothers of the other Churches, who have wished to take part in this celebration. May my most cordial greeting go to each one of them.

In this atmosphere of ecumenical charity we find a perfect place for the brief but so rich story of Blessed Maria Gabriella of Unity, whom I intentionally wanted to raise to the honors of the altar on this date and in this basilica. Her life, first through the Trappist vocation and then through the offering of her life for Christian unity, is totally expressed in these same three essential values: conversion, immolation for the brethren, prayer.

Nor could it have been otherwise. The Second Vatican Ecumenical Council, which in this very basilica and on this same date was announced by my venerated predecessor John XXIII, confirms this. In fact, on the subject of ecumenism, it is expressed in these precise terms: "There can be no ecumenism worthy of the name without a change of heart. For it is from newness of attitudes, from self-denial and unstinted love, that yearnings for unity take their rise and grow toward maturity. We should therefore pray to the divine Spirit for the grace to be genuinely self-denying, humble, gentle in the service of others, and to have an attitude of brotherly generosity toward them. . . . This change of heart and holiness of life, along with public and private prayer for the unity of Christians, should be regarded as the soul of the whole ecumenical movement, and can rightly be called 'spiritual ecumenism' " (Decree on Ecumenism, II, 7 and 8).

For that matter, St. John's whole chapter 17—that chapter whose pages were found yellowed by daily use in Sister Maria Gabriella's small personal Gospel book—is nothing other than the prayer erupting from the priestly heart of Christ, who, in the imminent prospect of the cross, implores conversion of heart for all who would believe in him.

4. I am happy to note, and to point out particularly to the young people, so fond of athletics and sports, that the young Trappist sister, to whom we attribute today for the first time the title of Blessed, was able to make her own the Apostle's exhortations to the faithful of Corinth (1 Cor 9:24) to "run so as to win," succeeding in the span of a few years — in the stadium of sanctity — to set a number of records that would make the most qualified champions envious. In fact, she is historically the first Blessed to come from the ranks of the Young Women of Catholic Action; the first among the young men and women of Sardinia; the first among Trappist nuns and monks; the first among workers in the service of unity. Four records set in the arena of that "school of divine service" proposed by the great Patriarch St. Benedict, which evidently is still valid even today after fifteen centuries, if it has been able to produce such examples of virtue in one who was able to accept it and put it into practice "with the mind of love."

In fact, it is precisely in this fidelity to listening that the young Maria Sagheddu — by nature stubborn and sharp, as witnesses and her own holy mother described her — was able to acquire that "conversion of heart" that St. Benedict asks of his children. Conversion of heart that is the true and primary source of unity.

From the moment when the obstinate and impetuous young little girl came in contact with the cross of Christ through the death of her favorite sister, she decided to surrender herself to him, docilely and humbly sought the guidance of a spiritual director, and agreed to involve herself in the life of the parish, joining the Young Women of Catholic Action, dedicating herself to the youngest children in catechesis, obliging to the elderly, spending hours in prayer. It is from that moment that that "conversion" began which accompanied her day by day, to the point of accepting the call to a vocation and leaving behind, when she was barely twenty-one, the beloved land and her dear ones of Sardinia, to present herself, heeding the voice of her divine Spouse, at the gates of the Trappists.

5. It is precisely this conversion of hers to God, this need of hers for unity in love, that constitutes the premise and the fertile

soil on which the Lord will make descend, at the set time, the call to total giving for the brethren.

The offering of her life for unity, which the Lord inspired in her during the week of prayer on these same days in 1938 — forty-five years ago — and which he showed pleased him like a fragrant holocaust of love, is not the start, but the finish of the young athlete's spiritual race. From the union achieved with the voice of God springs the movement of the Spirit to open herself to the brethren.

It is the discovery of the Vertical, of the Absolute of God, that gives meaning and effective urgency to the horizontal opening to the problems of the world. There is here a reminder, valuable today more than ever, against the easy temptation of a horizontal Christianity that would prescind from the search for the Vertex; the temptation of a psychologism that would ignore the mysterious presence and the unpredictable action of grace; the temptation of an activism that would begin and end only on an earthly level and perspective; the temptation of a brotherliness that would refuse to be illumined by a common divine father-hood.

It is from these premises that the heroic gesture of Sister Maria Gabriella surges to the heights of a great ecclesial event. Precisely because it is born from a sublime conversion directed toward the Father, her opening to the brethren identifies her with the crucified Christ, acquires historic value, and assumes ecumenical importance.

This leads us not only to admire and venerate, but also to reflect, to imitate, to study deeply, to suffer, and above all to pray, in order to root our way to conversion ever more in Christ.

So Blessed Maria Gabriella Sagheddu, who gracefully combines the names of the Angel of the Annunciation and the Virgin of the Acceptance, becomes a sign of the times and a model of that "spiritual ecumenism" of which the Council reminded us. She encourages us to look with optimism — over and above the inevitable difficulties that are ours as human beings — to the marvelous prospects of ecclesial unity, whose progressive verification is linked with the ever deeper desire to be converted to Christ, in order to make active and effective his yearning: *Ut omnes unum sint!* (That all may be one!).

Yes, Lord, may everyone soon succeed in being one. Along with us, she, the new Blessed, who spent her young life in joyful oblation in the flame of this divine yearning of yours, asks this of you.

Omnes...unum. Amen!

Hear Us, O Lord

How can one set a seal upon these pages in a manner most in accord with the person and spirit of Sister Maria Gabriella of Unity, if not by a moment of prayer in communion with the ideal of her life, the journey of her sanctity and the meaning of her immolation?

We do it by repeating here the six prayer intentions which were offered by the faithful in St. Paul's on January 25, and concluding as the Holy Father did that evening with the new liturgical prayer ("collect") in honor of the Blessed.

+ For our Holy Father John Paul II and all the Pastors of the universal church, for consecrated souls, for committed laity, that in the daily conversion to the love of Christ each one may realize, with the generosity of Paul, the Father's loving plan. We pray to the Lord.

+ For all believers in the God of Abraham, for all those who glory in the name of Christian, that under every heaven from east to west, made docile to the Spirit of the Father's Word, they may be efficacious laborers for unity and peace between the Churches and among peoples. We pray to the Lord.

+ For Christian families, that reliving the joyful experience of Cana and Bethany, they may grow in the warmth of divine intimacy and nourish through prayer the charism of the domestic church, open to the community of brothers and sisters and to the gift of vocations. We pray to the Lord.

+ For all those who suffer, for those deprived of the gift of faith and the comfort of hope, for broken families, for confused youth, for the oppressed and the oppressors, for those who love and those who hate, that the teaching of the Apostle and the charism of Blessed Maria Gabriella may be fruitful channels of unity and grace. We pray to the Lord.

+ That through the example of Blessed Maria Gabriella, worthy daughter of strong and generous Sardinia, the traditional religious, moral and family values of her people may be revived, and that through her intercession they may overcome the influences of violence and the temptations of evil. We pray to the Lord.

+ For all of us united at the tomb of St. Paul with the successor of Peter, that the intercession of the Queen of the Apostles may enable us to be faithful witnesses in word and in deed of the message of love and salvation of the one Christ, the Son of God. We pray to the Lord.

LET US PRAY,

O God, eternal Shepherd, who inspired Blessed Maria Gabriella, virgin, to offer her life for the unity of all Christians, grant that through her intercession, the day may be hastened in which all believers in Christ, gathered around the table of your Word and of your Bread, may praise you with one heart and one voice. Through Christ our Lord.